ASIN: B09842BDZJ

ISBN: 978-1-7778226-0-6

Cover design by: P.J. Restivo/Pixabay

Library of Congress Control Number: 2018675309

Printed in the United States of America

Contains some mature content.

For Bucky and all the kitties
and kitty lovers everywhere.

I'm so loveable.

Pre-Preface

She fell from Heaven and didn't break a bone.

Preface

She fell from Heaven and didn't break a bone
but tugged at my heart without breaking it
until the very end.

Post-Preface

She fell from Heaven and didn't break a bone
but tugged at my heart without breaking it
until the very end and I have not failed to
remember something about
her every day since.

Testimonials from the Famous

The smallest feline is a masterpiece.

Leonardo da Vinci

Time spent with cats is never wasted.

Sigmund Freud

Yeah. Yeah. My litter box needs cleaning.

H.R.B. Buckshot

Table of Contents

Pre-Preface..v

Preface..vi

Post-Preface..vii

Testimonials from the Famous viii

In the Beginning 4

But I Don't Want a Cat...8

Royal Name 12

Royal Provenance...14

The Stationery...17

The Royal Design 19

The Music..22

The Home Office..32

Saturday Morning Wakeup Call 34

A Cat's Worst Fear, V 1.0..36

Bucky Helps with Household Expenses 42

Great Corn Caper 46

WTF! To Do List..50

Date Rate..54

Let's Talk Ears...57

Getting There Was...60

Half the Fun..60

What the Hay!...68

Bucky's Higher Education..70

Tail-Chasing is Humiliating...72

Thinking Inside the Box...77

Toads – If it moves, it's mine! 82

Now a Word from a Sponsor – Plastic Cat Toys..........85

Catpeople..89

A Brush with Nature..92

DOS – macOS – WINDOWS - LINUX – APPLE iOS - BOS - 105

Pharaoh Faucet...112

Up the Down Staircase...123

Stately Anvil Manor..126

Spring Ahead. Fall Behind...131

NEWS ALERT..135

Unhampered..**136**

Always A Puzzle **148**

Afterword **158**

    PreLude *159*

    OrdinaryLude...*160*

    AfterLude *161*

    Post-AfterLude...*162*

Absolution Request...**163**

In the Beginning

There are times, many times, in fact, when storytelling must start at the beginning. Not the end. Not the middle. No flashbacks. This is one of those times. But I could be wrong.

Like many clear-thinking, loving people with a possibly-larger-than-desirable ego and craving for attention, I had little interest in a pet. That is, the part wherein I would own one and have it actually live in my home, would be particularly annoying. Sharing my living space. Making judgmental gestures about choices in creative projects, employers, rental apartments, house purchases, décor, gardening, financial investments, friends, romantic partners. Face it, truly, pets, especially certain kinds of pets, and you know the ones I mean. Them! So tiny. Quiet. Stalking you constantly from a safe and unnoticed distance. Eyeing you. Knowing without saying that they disapprove. Constantly weaseling their way into everything, absolutely everything you do. Again, you know their kind. There was just never going to be one of these creatures, these things, in my life. And, again, you know who or what I'm talking about here. Their kind. They all look alike. Need I say more.

Apparently, I do.

The Mother-in-Law

Do I really need to talk about my mother-in-law here? Ex-mother-in-law, to be precise. If you force me to do this, it will ooze to the surface questions about everything about me, some of which I recently mentioned in the page just before this one. It's right there. Can't miss it. If you've met the partner of your dreams and feel ready to make a commitment, you should really re-think this.

First, answer these all-important lifestyle questions:

1. Are you fond of listening to music loud enough to actually be heard?

2. Has the name Taylor Swift ever crossed your mind?

3. Do you feel you need to remember your partner's shoe size?

4. Have you seriously considered buying a sporty little Porsche?

5. Do you salivate uncontrollably at the mention of a 200-inch flatscreen with 97-channel surround sound featuring concrete-shattering subwoofers?

6. Do you begin to have tremors or temors the day before Valentine's Day?

7. Do the above-mentioned tremors or temors continue well into the following week because you failed to do something "Valentiney"?

8. Have you ever considered cooking something without a recipe?

9. Do you sometimes think about having just two pillows on your bed?

10. Do you trust your cat's judgement when it comes to mothers-in-law?

Number ten (10) is actually the critical question to ask yourself before such things as hiring a reception hall, caterer, florist, buying or renting formal wear, limos and other requirements for that perfect day and event. Number ten (10) suggests that everyone has a mother-in-law, even if it's just a rental unit.

It's a well-known fact that your proposed partner will have qualities handed down through the birth canal* and your cat is particularly good at sniffing out sour mothers-in-law. We've all seen little kitties circle the ankles of friends and guests in for a cocktail or two. Your cat, of course, is looking for clues - researching - possible acceptable relationships. Not for you, necessarily, but for itself, the little furry creature. If your cat dislikes the aroma (smell) and finds the ankles rough, irritable and otherwise unpleasant, heed this all-important tip: Cats are never wrong about these things.

I did not heed this all-important kitty advice.

But I Don't Want a Cat

Hello there. Would you like to switch your cell phone service or possibly adopt me?

I first had a cat in my life during graduate school in New York. You'd think a Vietnam veteran could see right through the plot. It was simple enough. I had the hots for a fellow grad babe and her cat was pregnant. Well, you get the picture. Love a new-born kitty and love the grad babe. She named it: Punnis. Said it was from the ancient Greek meaning a sweet, cuddly thing that will get you to at least second base. Naturally, none of that was true. Near as I could figure, "punnis", in Estonian, means an unsightly sore and grad babe was talking baseball – not dating.

A year or three later, Punnis lasted just two weeks in the marriage home – not the grade school babe and me, owing mostly to the mother-in-law's large, hairy, sheep dog that accompanied her on the too-often and controlling visits. With tears in my eyes,

I had to part with dear Punnis and hope she had a good life with her adoptive family.

But this is a story about the goddess Bucky. How did Bucky come to be my soul mate? As the title just above suggests. (Did you even bother reading it?) I didn't want another cat, no how, no way at all. This is when Fate stepped in. Fate had apparently been adequately sniffing my ankles and approved and sent a little ball of fur my way.

In this story, Fate shares the spotlight with Connecticut friends, Marty and Basia (M & B), who delegated care of their much-loved Papagena to yours truly. Papagena was named for a character in an opera by Mozart or Rossini or Randy Rainbow, but who can really tell because cats so rarely attend opera performances. Rather, they hang around backstage for the cast, musicians and audience to depart before beginning the nightly ritual of mouse hunting. Theater mice are known as thesbians*.

During an M & B absence, Papagena needed a regularly-scheduled VV (Vet Visit). She was very comfortable for the ten-minute drive over to the VVO (Vet Visit Office) and was pricelessly amenable to some pokes and stabs. A good kitty.

Before exiting, the vet, Dr. Thumbs Needleman, asked if I might be interested in a cat. Clearly, he had not read the title to this section, "But, I Don't Want a Cat", sending his Lovely VVO Assistant (LVVOA), Victoria Armstrong, to fetch Buckshot.

---

* Thesbian is a cross of the two words "thespian" and "lesbian" to describe two females nominated for a Golden Globe™, EMMY™ or OSCAR™ involved in the same theatrical production or film.

It's always an awkward moment when someone asks if you want to adopt one of their children, buy their teenage son's used car, attend a Tupperware party, consider an extended warranty for your recently-purchased electronic doorbell, or, in this case, take a puddy home.

The LVVOA stepped back into the office holding Buckshot and asked if I'd like to hold her. She was a very attractive LVVOA but I quickly realized she was referring to the puddy. I did not want a puddy and referred her to the title to this section: "But, I Don't Want a Cat." Was no one listening!

She pushed Buckshot into my chest forcing me to hold the critter in my arms. Big mistake.

" Buckshot's belly is all shaved and there appears to be sutures," I directed to Dr. Needleman.

"Of course. They are sutures. She was shot!"

"Oh. Buckshot. I get it now."

Buckshot was found along a nearby roadside, life passing from her sweet and fury body. Fate or luck stepped in. A passerby noticed the sweetie and took her to Dr. Needleman who saved her life.

"She's a princess!" he added.

With a tale like this, there was no hope of rejecting her. Home she came that day and was with me nearly fourteen years.

Danbury Daily Pancetta

World - Business - Finance - Lifestyle - Travel - Sport - Weather

All the news - from their house to your house

First Edition   Monday 5th June

Local Vet Saves Gunshot Victim
Hatter adopts

Extraordinary local Vet and his extraordinary Vet Assistant saved the life of what many are calling the most beautiful cat ever discovered.

Local unidentified resident played a small role by adopting the sweetie after multiple surgeries for gunshot wounds.

Victoria Armstrong (left) Dr. Thumbs Needleman and Buckshot

Unidentified adopter keeps injured kitty warm

*Hatter is a nickname for someone from Danbury, once known as the hat manufacturing capital of the U.S. Think Stetson (Stock file footnote/Footnotes for All Occasions.com.).

Royal Name

When you are partnered with an extraordinary pet, naming is important. While she came bundled with her own name, Princess Buckshot, I felt it was too long a name. For a royal, a name for casual use was needed, a nickname, especially among friends, family and neighbors was appropriate.

Buckshot and I had a considerable number of meetings on the issue. I scratched a few names on a napkin: Puddy, Pud, Kitty, Tiger, Sketch, Scratch, Ivanka, Wanderer, Wander, Meghan, Wonder, Paws. These met with contempt. But Princess Buckshot came to our conversations prepared with a PowerPoint presentation. It had just one slide.

It was perfectly obvious from the start. Her name was Buckshot. It was the only name she had ever had, she explained. "Don't tamper with a good thing," she said. "Besides, I'll rarely respond unless it's in my best interest."

I put forward the notion that Buckshot was kind of long and formal. Was there something shorter we could use. Hence, the great compromise: For all her formal communication (letters, memos, invitations, etc.), it would be HRB Buckshot – Her Royal Buckyness. For casual use at home, Bucky would be approved.

Royal Provenance

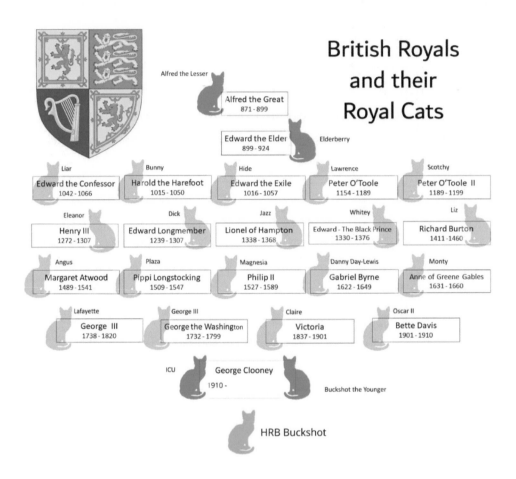

British Royals
and their
Royal Cats

Alfred the Lesser

Alfred the Great
871 - 899

Edward the Elder
899 - 924
Elderberry

| Liar | Bunny | Hide | Lawrence | Scotchy |
| Edward the Confessor 1042 - 1066 | Harold the Harefoot 1015 - 1050 | Edward the Exile 1016 - 1057 | Peter O'Toole 1154 - 1189 | Peter O'Toole II 1189 - 1199 |

| Eleanor | Dick | Jazz | Whitey | Liz |
| Henry III 1272 - 1307 | Edward Longmember 1239 - 1307 | Lionel of Hampton 1338 - 1368 | Edward - The Black Prince 1330 - 1376 | Richard Burton 1411 - 1460 |

| Angus | Plaza | Magnesia | Danny Day-Lewis | Monty |
| Margaret Atwood 1489 - 1541 | Pippi Longstocking 1509 - 1547 | Philip II 1527 - 1589 | Gabriel Byrne 1622 - 1649 | Anne of Greene Gables 1631 - 1660 |

| Lafayette | George III | Claire | Oscar II |
| George III 1738 - 1820 | George the Washington 1732 - 1799 | Victoria 1837 - 1901 | Bette Davis 1901 - 1910 |

ICU

George Clooney
1910 -
Buckshot the Younger

HRB Buckshot

To claim royalty, though, I explained that she might, at some time by some person, be asked to prove her aristocratic standing. I mean, you just can't go around telling people you are of royal blood, unless you are Anastasia of Russia living in Virginia. It's called provenance, a lengthy and deep research project first developed in a well-known Rhode Island city, often requiring upwards of days to complete. Fortunately, these days we have online helpers such as:

- AncestryYourCreditCard.com;
- MormonsRochesterNewYork.com;
- PrincessDiannaRelativesEverywhere.com;

as well as many other useful resources regularly advertised on Fox News.

Right here and now, let me assure readers that an exhaustive study of the challenge and split-infinitives was made resulting in fascinating new knowledge. For example, it was heretofore* not widely known that royal cats were the first to introduce kings and queens to the idea of the chamber pot so common today in royal households.

* (Not a real footnote) Before I learned the correct meaning of "heretofore", I thought it was some kind of toe disorder.

* Thesbian, you'll recall from a previous footnote, is a cross of the two words "thespian" and "lesbian" to describe two females nominated for a Golden Globe, EMMY or OSCAR involved in the same theatrical production or film. Some have texted to inquire further.

** Originally from the Latin "The Spians" meaning a group of one or more people who could not correctly spell the word "Spain".

(The formatting of footnotes here is suggested in the new board game *Fun with Footnotes.*)

As easily seen in the nearby ancestry chart, every king and/or queen and/or consort******* held their household pets close with superior accommodation, attention and frolicking.****

It was not uncommon, for example, for royalty and cat to use their respective chamber pots at the same time. This would sometimes kick up some dust or powder from which we get several of today's common phrases such as "powder room" and "taking a powder" and "keep your powder dry." Meanwhile   in Scotland, Scotspeople, or kilters, as they are best known, were practicing a bizarre ritual with their dogs known as *The Wheelbarrow*. You'll need to Google this one yourselves. Bucky and I would be far too embarrassed to explain and we are far too polite to even use an asterisk with this fact.

Moving ahead, truly, the kitties were recognized as a loving part of the royal families of Britain.

So, then, by now you've read and analyzed the ancestry chart, and we can all readily acknowledge that our Buckshot, HRB, is a direct descendent of the pairing of Alfred the Lesser and Elderberry, and eventually, ICU (pronounced *eye – see – you*) and Buckshot the Younger.

Yes. This will be on the final.

**** From the German meaning "wife" and English meaning "licking". (This footnote was too embarrassed to be seen with the others.)

******* I've lost track of the footnotes. "Consort" is a musical term used to describe a group of musicians intimate with a king and/queen.

The Stationery

The United Kingdom or Britain, or Great Britain, or Not Scotland, or seldom thought of, Not Ireland, is the realm of the Royal Family. By that I mean the Queen or King. By that I mean Elizabeth or George Clooney, and certainly not Harry who is now the Fresh Prince of Bel-Air.

Royalty needs to communicate with subjects of the realm. For this, many experts recommend stationery or, what some term paper. For this chore one sends the Royal Household Executive Secretary (RHES) to a reputable stationer, a designer and printer of paper products for use outside the Royal Bathroom (RB) or Commode Abode (CA).

Since 1887-ish, Smythson (pronounced *SMEYETH – SON* or in New York, *SMIT-TIE'S*) - at London's fashionable Bond Street, has been the stationer (meaning it has not moved) to many of London's most famous detectives and spies and exotic fashion models, and to the Royal Family. For a sum of money too large to publish, Smythson will provide a magnificent royal design for writing paper, envelopes, note pads, pens, pencils, calendars, stamps and other royal necessaries. While the price tag on the many offerings is through the roof, there are two important positives to keep in mind:

First, the British value their currency in pounds - not dollars. This is extremely convenient for those of us who still use our fingers and toes to count. If royal stationery costs, say, 1,200 pounds for fifty sheets, simply count out your dollars on a kitchen or bathroom scale until the display reads 1,200 pounds.

Second, Smythson's shop is awesome and as quaint and picturesque as you would imagine; so, a visit is a dress up occasion. These days, recently-pressed jeans are fine with a gold-buttoned blue blazer, expensive button-down shirt and member-of-parliament-style tie and shoes that appear recently polished by a manservant – known in France as a serviette. FYI, ladies, they also sell shoes, handbags and a wide variety of Bond Street wares.

The Royal Design

Truth be known, HRB Buckshot's communication needs are modest. Naturally, she needed letter-size correspondence sheets, matching envelopes, a business card and, of course, a custom postage stamp.

The business card required the most attention. Why a business card? Her Buckyness, while royalty, still needed a job. Harry and Meghan fully understand this. So, the card had to be regal and informative with an easy reading style. This was not as easy a challenge as you might suppose.

The Business Card

The Letterhead

Her Royal Buckyness

Salmo quæ incedunt quadrupedia, et usque in sempiternum

By appointment only
Buckyness Palace
HRBBuckshot7@gmail.com

The Envelope

Her Royal Buckyness
Buckyness Palace

The Royal Postage Stamp

The Music

Tropical fish do not hear music! This is a little-known fact. Fact is, fish are not bright. The average fish, and I am not making this up, has a memory span of just three seconds. Face it, fish don't even know they are wet.

Many four-legged creatures hear music simply as noise. Again, this is true. This doesn't make them inferior; it may simply be that they've only been exposed to Motorhead, Anthrax, Slipknot, Machine Head, Sodom, Alice in Chains, Napalm Death, Disturbed, Ratt, I've Been There and It Sucks, Capn' Crunch in Hell, No Saints in St. Louis, Mud is Dirty and Wet and, well, you get the idea.

Dating way back to early times when the turntable was invented, in the Egyptian era, circa 1923, it was well established that cats, revered as the gods they were, listened to and loved music.

The Pharaohs, gods themselves, could afford musicians to play for the royal courts. Their cats loved this. Ordinary people, however, had to rely on recordings made on round disks made of clay – the same kind of clay used to make vases, except that these disks were scribed by the business end of a rhinoceros horn while spinning on a slave-powered wagon wheel. These devices magically preserved sound. Many are available today at Pottery Barn.

While all cats can be genetically traced to Egypt where their mother ship first landed, Bucky's lineage can be traced only to 891 CE and Alfred the Great's cat, Alfred the Lesser, when music skills were permanently imprinted somewhere between her two ears. MRIs, to date, however, have proved inconclusive.

It was a dark and stormy winter night in 1990. It really was. Neighbors in my Long Beach, Long Island, apartment building dropped around after work for wine and cheese. I prepared the wine and Bucky prepared the cheese. Just six, two-legged creatures sitting around listening to some Dave Brubeck on the turntable. Three couples. Women comparing rings. Guys staring at knees anxiously awaiting summer.

Speaking for myself, one of the more annoying things cats do is this constant picking at carpets, curtains, pretty much anything they can get their claws into. It's a perfectly natural activity, though. Cats were designed to annoy us whenever possible. It's a tactic perfected back in the Egyptian era when kitties needed attention and spied the pharaoh's nine-million-NeferNub* Persian carpet.

---

* A NeferNub is not a cosmetic but a unit of ancient Egyptian currency approximately equal to ten bazillion, present-day U.S. dollars.

Bucky was not exceptional in this regard. What was exceptional was her taste in music. Music? Claws?

After hours of toing and froing reading the spine labels on all bottom shelf LPs. One caught her attention.

Some background here. I had nearly four-thousand LPs. Yes. Four-thousand or, more accurately: 4,000. That's nearly the length of three metric-sized Olympic pools. *

* Measuring an Olympic-sized pool, by the way, has been accomplish only by Schrödinger's cat.

But I digress.

The album she favored was one I received in the years when a teen and lifetime member of the Columbia Record Club – Columbia House.

If you are too young to know about such clubs or to old to remember them, this club would send you twelve free LPs if you signed up to receive one new LP each month until approximately when the cows come home. Should you be away for any reason when the cows came home, the club sent an IBM card** warning that the month's selection, usually *Percy Faith Plays the Music of Elvis,* * would be sent unless the card was returned within 18-hours of receipt.

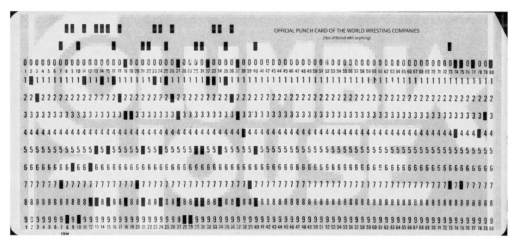

OFFICIAL PUNCH CARD OF THE WORLD WRESTING COMPANIES
(Not affiliated with anything)

* Percy Faith was the world's most popular instrumental orchestra leader using actual instruments. He was Columbia Records' biggest attraction and a Canadian to boot. A lesser-day Yanni.

** The IBM punch card was a clever paper alternative to all the plastic stuff needed to transact modern day purchases. Cards the size of your basic No.10 envelope were filled with little holes punched by a staff of nearly 3.7 million workers at IBM plants in Albuquerque, New Mexico; Florence, North Carolina; and Patchogue, New York. Each hole represented an important element of your financial transaction. Holes might include: your name, address, phone number, social security number, blood type, shoe size, mom's maiden name, elementary school teacher names, coffee preferences and, of course, album title. This paper alternative to plastics was soundly rejected by industry leaders because it favored tree cutting over plastics farming.

But I digress.

The album.

Working for more than an hour picking away at the album spine, Bucky successfully released the LP, allowing it to fall to the floor, front side up. (Persons born before 1985 know an LP album jacket is roughly 12 inches by 12 inches, somewhat larger than a sheet of ordinary printer paper.) Bucky spent the next five minutes standing on the record cover and circling within its edges. Each way around lowering her body until it was in a tight, soft cuddle position. This was followed by a decisive "meow".

Oh yes. The album title.

So, we played the album on the made-in-Denmark Bang & Olufsen turntable. It was a wonderful sound and experience I somehow overlooked these many years. Zamfir, known to his mom as Gheorghe (Georgie), has a great sound on an instrument I only played at Halloween, made of orange, sugared gummy wax.

WOWEE, Buffalo, NY

The Wowee wax gum whistle/harmonica was featured in the movie *Valley Girl*. Nicolas Cage played it in an effort to symbolize the "blues" for his girlfriend.

Kids loved it.

Dentists adored it.

Please note here that the Wowee wax gum whistle harmonica cannot be played while wearing the complementary wax lips.

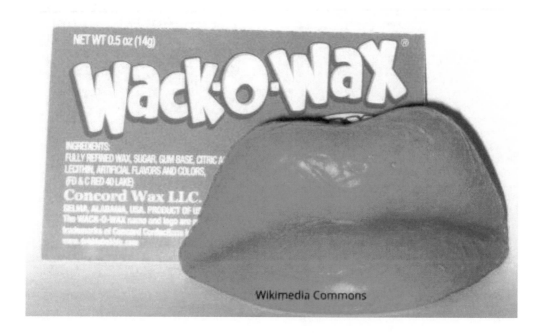

Wikimedia Commons

Wowee was the Buffalo, New York-based candy company some 65 years in the confectionery business (Now a division of W&F Manufacturing, Glenn Confections, Inc. or Amazon).

It is widely assumed the model for the wax lips was Hollywood horror movie star, Bel Lugosi. This is unproven in a court of law.

Bela Lugosi as Dracula in the
Universal Pictures series.

But I digress.

From that memorable Bang & Olufsen (B&O) - not to be confused with the bankrupt American railroad now a prominent part of many U.S. Monopoly board games - moment, Bucky's Halloween card featured a reference to the great musician.

I just love Zamfir!
HRB Bucky

The Home Office

With Her Royal Buckyness now having a fully authenticated title, work began to secure her home office. "You have a home office why shouldn't I," she argued with just the slightest edge of demand.

Aided by interior decorator Hans Foote, countless meetings were held. Bucky's needs became clear. Nothing fancy.

- Traditional style over utility.
- A medium-size room with barristers filled with
    Moroccan-leather-bound collectable books covering
    all but one wall. Bucky was never a voracious reader
    but she did enjoy scratching book bindings.
- One window with ample sill for napping on sunny days.
- One 1950s vintage phone that rings periodically but
    not connected to anything.
- One computer keyboard not attached to anything for the
    aiming of hairballs.
- Small passthrough from her office to mine for those
    times she might want to visit.

Saturday Morning Wakeup Call

If you're anything like me, you relish Saturday morning sleep-ins. Noon is a civilized time for breakfast after a week's hard work. Though beautiful, it's fun not seeing the sun rising every single day. We're talkin' before the crack of dawn. Not pulling a pillow over ears blocking the sound of the Black & Decker automatic coffee maker beginning its annoying workday drip routine. (Why didn't B & D stick to making drills and saws.) Not dragging weary bones to the shower at sunrise.   Not inhaling the caffeine-laden oxygen aroma of coffee dripping into the carafe. If only kitties fully understood what we have to deal with.

They do not! And Bucky was no exception.

She'd jump up at the foot of the bed and agonizingly slowly, stepping on my legs, padding her way up the bed to the pillow. Finding I had pulled the covers over my head, she'd scratch away trying to find some little opening she could get a paw into. Failing that, it was back to the foot of the bed, picking at the blanket and sheets until an opening had been created and working herself under the covers to my head where she would pause before taking the tip of my nose into her mouth. Not a bite at all. Just holding my nose long enough to discover I really do not like tuna breath all that much. It was an effective strategy, she learned, and I discovered in the best-seller, *It's a Cat's Life, Not Yours* by Emily Scratching-Post Smythe.

A Cat's Worst Fear, V 1.0

Felix/Dreamstime/PJR/YouTube

A cat's worst fears: a world without mice and butterflies, sofas and pillows and living room furniture, homes with no crawl space under beds, two felines sharing the same litter box. ("Excuse me, I believe I had a reservation."), humans expecting to play after 4 pm, humans who don't expect to play after midnight. So many fears.

I found the worst possible cat fear - totally Freddy Kruger-scary - is an unexpected one, unimaginable actually: WD-40. Yes. WD-40. The very same chemical product widely used to prevent jet engine corrosion, rust on cars, sticky hinges everywhere. WD-40.

Many believe WD-40 is to things mechanical as aspirin is to human aches, pains, income taxes. To Bucky it was more. Much more. WD-40 was the Hiroshima, the Nagasaki, the Donald Trump of cat-astraphies.

Guys, you know that sometimes things just seem to happen. Most often without warning or explanation. Things that cannot be fixed with duct tape, the universal adapter.

Turning over in our bed, the only actually store-assembled furniture in our new Connecticut house, the first thing the wife says to me is, "Don't you ever call me 'the wife'." Figuring the night of possible romance had come to a swift and deflated end, I turned over again to find comfort and sleep on my side of the bed. Wrong. Bucky was there with her face in my face. True, it's difficult to tell when cats are laughing at us, but I was sure she was.

"And furthermore, I expect you to finish the living room painting and vacuum the mess," my honey, sweetie, love of my life, commanded.

"If I promise all these things, will there be lovemaking in our lives tonight?"

"Only if you love yourself, dear. It's not your birthday."

Next morning, after some vitamin E had been applied to soothe the chafing, I finished the living room sanding and painting.

Then, the cleanup.

Guys know machinery. Anything that can be done by hand can be better done by machine. This is why the coin operated "Your Wife Way from Home" machine in diner men's restrooms worldwide became so popular for about a week in August,

1958. For those not familiar with this almost-huge financial and pleasure success, a description might be in order.

Jeff Boyce/Wikimedia Commons

"Your Wife Away from Home" was a vending machine-like unit fixed to restroom walls in a number of otherwise respectable, mostly-interstate highway diners, near relatively lonely towns where, at one time in history, travelling salesmen, for example, would have a lonely meal at a lonely counter, and after an apple pie à la mode or alamode or ala mode and coffee, would discover a need for relief, a la commode. After wandering into the men's room and doing what was needed, it was noticed that a vending machine-like device was attached to a wall near the exit. Did I mention that men are fascinated by machine-like devices?

It is rumored there are some women who share this fascination. Naturally, men dismiss the notion that women are curious about machine-like devices as they are mothers of our children. That doesn't stop men. Curious as we are, as Columbus and those pesky Vikings were, we'd notice a vending machine-like device affixed to a rest room wall with the sign, "Your Wife Away from Home – 50 Cents." Geeez, we'd think, what could possibly go wrong with a vending machine-like device on the wall of the men's room for 50 cents. There it is. A metal box with a slot for coins and a hole for… well, you know what. Who could possibly resist? This could be the 50-cent Barbarella. So, as God intended, we'd put *it* into this strange device on the wall, insert the coins and scream out in pain only a cat can imagine as we withdraw the heretofore unnamed biological unit, bloody, racked with pain and a button sewn on the end. That's pain and fear!

So, where does WD-40 fit into this story?

First, WD-40 is a magnificent trade-marked product made by wonderful people represented by a clowder of lawyers.

If my romantic, my hormonal (and, mind you, even scientists, have never made a whore moan without upfront cash), intentions had succeeded, I would never have considered lubricating my jammed Kenmore rug beater attachment with a spray of WD-40. Have you ever sprayed WD-40 into anything electrical while actually operating? If you have, then you were likely as dense and sex-deprived as I was.

Ladies, if you are not acquainted with WD-40, you'll be relieved to know it's a great product if used according to directions. You've probably walked right by it, sitting on that shelf at your local motorcycle parts store.

39

I thought quality lubrication was the answer to all resistance. You know what I mean. So, while the Now-Defunct-Sears-Kenmore-Canister-like unit was trying its best to suck the dust from the living room carpet, I sprayed just a tiny bit of WD-40 into the base of the beater attachment. It was a tiny bit of WD-40, but just enough to remind this Sears device that WD-40 and electrical sparks don't get along well. If I had read the label with the required 30X magnifying glass, I would have seen: *CAUTION. Do not spray WD-40 into Sears Kenmore vacuum cleaners unless you are a complete idiot.*

Clearly Bucky had better reflexes than I. She vacated the room, all rooms, and stashed herself under the 500-gallon oil tank in the basement for four days. The Kenmore exploded! Mind you, I served America, if not well, at least vulnerably, in Vietnam. The assault on the Kenmore beachhead was worse. An explosion even combats veterans and slacker, Foot-Spurs Trump, could not imagine. Deafening the noise was. Sparks shooting out the Kenmore anus. Bucky, a flash of lightning leaving the room faster than you could spell "E X I T." I've seen military jets that don't move that fast. If John Wayne were still with us, he'd be making a combat movie about it - *The Fighting WD-40th!*

Bucky Helps with Household Expenses

How many times have we emptied the dryer lint filter? I figure somewhere between once and 6,000 times. How many times have you thought about where all this lint goes? I figure between none and once. During a brief period of unemployment – or, as we prefer to say, freelancing, I couldn't help but observe that at least fifty-percent of all dryer lint is actually cat hair.

So, I had the discussion with HRB Buckshot, Her Royalness.

PJ: "Sweetie, are you aware of just how much of your hair ends up on my clothing, towels, T-shirts, etc.?"

HRB: "Why would I notice or care?"

PJ: "Well, it's yours."

HRB: "Once it leaves me, it's yours. I thought that was clear from the start."

PJ: "But there's so much in the dryer."

HRB: "Not all of it. Some's on your keyboard in the form of a hair ball."

PJ: "During these difficult financial times, do you think there's something you can do to help out with some extra cash?"

HRB: "No. What ever gave you that idea? Does it even look like I have pockets?"

Bucky had never really taken an interest in laundry or the laundry room which is actually in the garage, home of that big oily-smelling thing with dirty wheels that leaves backwards but at least must know the secret code that opens the garage door.

So, one lazy Saturday evening, I interrupted the puddy's regularly-scheduled 8 – 9 PM nap to demonstrate the dryer filter. I'm certain she was amazed, maybe startled, by the hair I had collected apparently from some other cat I'd somehow secreted away. That was the accusation.

43

PJR: "It's yours. All yours, sweetie."

HRB. "You've had it DNA tested then?"

I explained my plan. Bucky would continue to do her part in providing hair but in greater quantities. I would collect it using various household implements. The dryer, of course. Forks. Clothing brushes. Vacuum (once I bought a new one). Then, together we would find a way to spin it into commercially valuable yarn.

Googling "cat yarn", I discovered what lots of keen entrepreneurs seemingly have known for decades. Kitty yarn and anything knitted from kitty yarn is in high demand by at least several people worldwide. Sweaters, scarfs, mittens, hats, fancy Christmas tree ornaments. The list goes on. Bucky and I would make our mark and cash-in big time.

Hardly a day went by that I didn't brush the sweetie at least twice, collecting scads of valuable resource material for our new venture. Brushings, carpet sweepings and dryer filter dregs. After just one week's time we had collected upwards of one kilo – the equivalent of a small ball of yarn. A retail market value of some $5. Bucky was not impressed. It was the hardest work – actually, the only work – she had ever done and was simply not going to cooperate further.

Saturday morning, I woke to what was once a neat $5 ball of yarn trailing around the house: upstairs, downstairs, around furniture, around kitchen chairs, ending in a comfy bundle near her food service center.

Plan B: Send out more resumes.

Great Corn Caper

So, you never thought of corn as having a caper. Perhaps, like so many of us, until it happens, of course, you were thinking corn cob. No. This was a *corn caper*.

First, you've got to be kidding when you say not everyone likes or eats corn. Corn, in some way, is in just about everything we eat. True. That Pepsi in your left hand is sweetened with corn syrup. Where do they get corn syrup? From corn. Even vegans, rare creatures from the planet Vega, believed to have travelled to Earth in the 1950s, will tolerate corn if Marmite is in short supply. Marmite, pronounced *yuk-key*, is made by squeezing the life out of yeast and, allegedly, worn shoe soles (WSS).

There are many ways to enjoy corn: creamed from a can is not one of them. I had an early lesson in tooth care. One set of grandparents had lost all their teeth early in life to Mr. Tooth Decay due to poor oral hygiene and possibly too much Marmite before bedtime. This was not just tooth loss. It was teeth loss. These kind people were condemned to a life of canned, creamed corn. Lesson learned. So, we are agreed then: floss and brush often and corn from the cob will be your reward.

OK. So, corn. It contains some life essentials, even for cats: These include protein, minerals and great flavor. However, not all corn products are good for animals. Not that I would ever refer, even jokingly, to Bucky as an animal. (In New Jersey, it's *am-in-al*.) Corn is often used as a filler in processed foods, even pet foods. Processed corn, though, anything from a package or can, could contain certain seasonings cats may find toxic. Check with your vet for a better understanding of CC, cat corn.

But I digress.

Over time, cats, being the delightfully- and annoyingly-curious love sponges they are, will discover their corn likes and dislikes. That's the way it was with HRB.

Living on my own for a number of years, there was no need for some typical home dining conventions. Guys, you know the ones I mean. Where is it written that pants, for example, must be worn to dinner? Nowhere! Where is it written that you cannot enjoy a dinner sitting on the floor, meal plates on a coffee table and professional wrestling on the TV? Not you, of course, wrestling on top of the TV, but two bozos with names like Gargantua and Captain Codice Piece. Nowhere is it written!

That's the way it was one sultry July evening. Backyard-grilled burger. A slice of lettuce. A slice of tomato. Not so much lettuce and tomato as to confuse the burger into believing it is actually a rogue salad. French's ketchup. A lightly-toasted bun. A piece of corn on the cob, a Moosehead beer from Canada.

The kitchen phone rings. (You'll have to imagine a ring here.) My aching back rises and I stumble to the kitchen wall phone. (Clearly this was in an era when phones and walls were not as mobile as today's modern units.) Chatting away, from the corner of an eye, I spot a crime in the making. Bucky is dragging my cob of corn down the hallway.

At this point there may be value in explaining why I say cob instead of ear. The two terms are often used interchangeably by less-informed people and dogs. An ear is a cob that includes the silk and husks. Cats know this.

But I digress.

"Gotta run. Call ya back in an hour."

As quickly and as quietly as I could, I tippy-toed or actually padded to the kitchen doorway and peeked. There she was. HRB Buckshot, Her Royal Buckyness, dragging a cob of corn, her prey, down the hall to the bedroom.

Next, there she is under the bed, both paws on the cob. Digging her eye teeth into the kernels and licking the syrup.

Have you ever wondered why *kernel* and *colonel* are pronounced similarly? Shouldn't at least one of these words be pronounced *colon-el*?

But I digress, again.

Naturally, I had to get down on the floor. Her level. And watch her at work. Each time I moved a half-inch closer, she pawed the cob closer to herself.

Now, when corn is to be had for a meal, I break off a piece from an end and give it to her. In summer, she too often smells like she just came from the movie theater.

The Great Corn Caper.

WTF! To Do List

Cats are busy at all times. Sure, it may not appear this way, but busyness is really in the mind of the beholder, isn't it?

Like so many other kitties, Bucky works just three days each week: Wednesday, Thursday, Friday (WTF).

WEDNESDAY	
12:17 am	Pad lightly to the kitchen. Smack something. Make a noise.
12:37 am	Pad lightly to the living room
12:48 am	Drag whatever was used to make the living room noise to the dining room. Make a noise.
1:12 am	Scratch hard and noisily in litter box even if you do not need to use it.
1: 32 am	Jump up and flick the staircase 3-way light switch on.
1:34 am	Run up the stairs and flick the staircase 3-way light switch off.
1:47 am	Run down the stairs and flick the staircase 3-way light switch on.
2:09 am	Run up the stairs and flick the staircase 3-way light switch off. Repeat as often as necessary.
3:14 am	Be certain Peter is asleep, quietly make your way to the laundry hamper. Remove all underwear. Drag underwear to secret hiding place behind the entertainment center. Rest.

More WTF...

WEDNESDAY	Continued
7:15 am	As Peter walks to the door on his way out to work, bite and hold onto his pant leg.
7:30 am	Walk around the house twice just to be certain nothing has changed in the last hour.
9:00 am	Paw your nose at food bowl leftovers
9:15 am	Stare out dining room window.
12:23 pm	Check litterbox.
12:40 pm	Turn on stereo sound system and listen to Zamfir album on the turntable, Jump onto the sofa and nap.
1:37 pm	Wind the grandfather clock in the den.
1:43 pm	Early afternoon nap.
2:37 pm	Unravel as much toilet paper as possible before the upcoming nap.

More WTF...

THURSDAY	
	Ditto. Or, if you are not well informed, you must like dogs. This is not a terrible thing. So many dogs love my company, especially when they, too, are napping.
FRIDAY	
	Ditto. Or, if you are not well informed, again, you must like dogs. This is not a terrible thing. So many dogs love my company, especially when they, too, are napping.
SATURDAY,	**SUNDAY, MONDAY, TUESDAY**
	"These words feel familiar. Where have I seen them before? Are they relevant to my life? Were these special meal days? Was *60 Minutes* on one of these days? Is Mike Wallace still on *60 Minutes?*" - Bucky

Date Rate
Waiting for Go-doo

Tomasz Leśniowski/Wikimedia Commons/Dreamstime

Now, I know how Michael Douglas endured his term as President of the United States. That was briefly back in 1995. Sure. He was widowed and lonely and what do you do if you are President? Yes. You meet Annette Benning, a lobbyist who makes good and the President.

But the thing here is that it's not easy to do the ordinary things people do when you are a major public figure.

Romance? Yikes! But in those secret moments when climbing the White House stairs to the White House bedroom to the White House bed, Michael Douglas had one thing most of the rest of us do not: The Secret Service. This elite presidential protection arm of the federal government was created in 1865 as the United States Secret Service (USSS), a branch of the U.S. Treasury Department. It's first mandate was to stop the counterfeiting of currency. This it agreed to do. Others did not. Later assignments included personal protection of the President and members of Congress. We are quite certain the USSS, as it was known early on, probably could not imagine its agents' secrecy skills applied to a president's need for late-night pillow fluffing with a woman not his wife. Imagine, too, if you are the teenage son or daughter of the president and, as teens are wont to do, they bring a date home after the prom. The scene was wonderfully brought to life by composer Irving Berlin in his 1962 Broadway musical, *Mr. President*. The president's young daughter wants a romantic evening with a newly-discovered love. Just when she's ready to kiss him, the Secret Service agent pops up from behind the sofa leading to the song "The Secret Service Makes Me Nervous."

As you can see from my imagined New York apartment staircase to heaven pictured on a nearby page, my "Secret Service" agent was a tabby.

Bucky, of course, who, on date evenings donned her official red COPS ball cap and stationed herself near the first step of the staircase, or, as she liked to call it, First Base. COPS? Cat on Patrol Service.

From her special vantage point, she could size up my final candidate for date night as we climbed to what was named the "One-in-a-Million-Chance-of-Marriage Suite."

Next morning, we always knew Bucky's take on the date. A clean bottom stair step and all was well. A loving poop deposit on the bottom step meant a step down to "eliminated" in the Bucky rating system.

Let's Talk Ears

Photo by Joanna Zaleska

A few chapters back, you likely noticed or breezed over Bucky's activity chart – the WTF - noticing, perhaps, that naps are an important part of her day. The chart and, indeed, our casual observation, would suggest that there is little-to-nothing happening during kitty naps and deep-sleep episodes. This is a conclusion is tragic human mistake and hugely unfair for the reputation of these divine creatures.

Scientists and animal (pronounced, once again, *am-in-al* in New Jersey) behaviorists have long believed in using hyphens sparingly and that a cat's keen sense of hearing continues unrelentingly even during the deepest snooze.

No doubt you've observed that a cat's ears twitch at the sound of a can opener just when you thought they had passed out for a few days' napping. This is but one example of their tiny but adorable brains alert to sounds of food that could be theirs. In the wild, this same characteristic protects felines from approaching predators.

Unique, perhaps, Bucky's ears can turn 180 degrees and can achieve this feat independently of each other. This led to a remarkable, if not brief, career in show business at Dolby Laboratories in Hollywood.

Dolby, you'll recognize as a pillar of the motion picture, professional and home recording industries – as in Dolby Stereo, etc.

It wasn't founder Ray Dolby himself but a close associate, perhaps in shipping, who put out the call for cat research study volunteers.

Hollywood Auditions

World-renowned movie industry giant seeks talented, reliable, photogenic, playful, patient, scientifically curious cat for study of stereo sound. Must be at least two years old but less than four, with parental consent, in very good health, GED and strong respect for its owner - if not, any cat will do.

CONTACT Ray Dolby - yes, that Dolby, at giant_stereo@dolbylabz. com.

(Dogs need not apply.)

It was a forgone conclusion that Dolby would select Bucky as its principal test subject, if only on the basis that she is the cutest ever and possibly the only kitty with a GED, to respond.

Getting There Was
Half the Fun

Many readers will have had some experience travelling with their kitty, if only down the street to the vet by car, or as British kitties say, "The Motor." Lots of meows and other words that cannot be mentioned in polite company. For Bucky, the trial was not travel by car but travel by air. Just saying the word "airplane" or, as she likes to say, "the aero", and she'd run for cover under the bed. Cars – the motor – she loves.

Los Angeles is a long way from home, some three-thousand miles, or forty-five thousand kilometers. A much-too-long drive to handle on her own. So, against my better judgement, I agreed to share the driving. This was particularly important as I would be the only driver with a license.

We loaded the Honda Civic with snacks, water, litterbox and off we went on a bright, sunny, warm, sultry Connecticut Sunday in May. Important stops along the way – well, not actually along the way - included Catsburg, North Carolina; Cat Springs, Texas; and Los Gatos, California. I succumbed to Bucky's logic that this may be the only time we'd be able to experience these special places.

Pulled over by the Texas Highway Patrol just outside Cat Springs for an alleged distracted driving violation, officer Billy Bo Boulder (his real name) asked, "What's that thing around your neck?" I explained it was a cat. With a quizzical look on his sun-parched, creviced face, he politely asked, "That thing alive or ya want me to shoot it for you?"

Officer Billy Bo let us go with just a warning this time muttering something about F_ _ ing litterbox-hugging Obama lovers. Bucky and I figured our best course of action was a slow move ahead until just outside of gunshot range heading to the much-sought-after Cat Springs where we could pause, rest, open a can of salmon* and enjoy cat-related activities.

* If "salmon" is pronounced *sa-mon*, why isn't "colonel" pronounced *co -nel*?

Next, the historic and iconic Cat Springs sign we had read so much about.

Nestled in the flat, dusty land surrounded by Highways 1457, 159, 109,1094, 71, 290, 36 and Intestate 10, just 60 miles from Houston and light years from San Antonio, Cat Springs is well-known for hospitality that surpasses even that of nearby New Ulm, Texas.

First stop, the Catnip Café, a picturesque look back at the old American south, or, as locals put it today, home to all who walk on two or four feet.

The Catnip Café is centrally located off Highway 949 just a short walk from the Sunset Cottage B & B, the Reichardt Company

Cattle Holding Pens where we saw few cattle held by people, and the United States Post Office whose sign read, "We Stamp Good."

It was a much-needed rest stop - bathroom and refreshments. Bucky used a privacy-style litterbox inside and I was directed to an elm tree out back. The building dates to 1921 when wood was the chief construction material and lists ever so slightly to starboard.

The Catnip offered a wide variety kitty-related necessities including balls of yarn, snack-size cans of tuna and salmon and, naturally, locally sourced organic catnip.

Purchases: Science Diet, Doritos, an emergency flare and, to prove we had actually been to Texas, a package of chewing tobacco (pronounced *chaw–in ta-back-ee*).

Leaving historic and, not to mention, beautiful Cat Springs, we encountered a road sign.

Hollywood

The actual, scientifically arguable diagram somewhere below illustrates just one hearing study finding. Cats have an amazing sense of hearing such that they can actually distinguish different sounds just a few inches apart at distances up to five feet. I am not making this up.

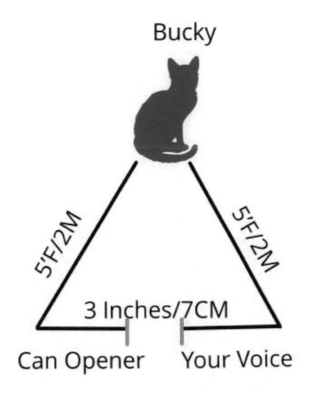

Add to this, the ability to hear sounds so soft that they are beyond a human's puny ability. Bucky's hearing is nearly five-times greater than mine. When was the last time you heard a candle lit in a distant room? Bucky's hearing is nearly five-times greater than ours. Oh. I think I've already mentioned this.

More recent studies at Catswald Collegiate Institute, a prestigious university in Scotland, a small but charming country, best known for its sweaters-without-buttons industry, suggests cats can hear multi-direction sound even from one ear. Placing this in perspective, humans require a minimum of six ears to achieve a result barely approaching what Bucky and her friends can do from birth.

Bucky, like most cats, can capture sound from all directions with each ear. It's like 360-degree stereo times two ears.

So, next time you're at a big movie theater and you are able to discern a roaring car on the left and Julia Roberts' teeth grinding on the right, you'll know Bucky had a paw in all this Dolby Stereo.

What the Hay!

We all have our own brand of weed, a college buddy once told me. For Bucky, for a time, a short time, it was hay. You'd think it would be catnip. Well, it still is catnip but for three days one summer in Georgia, it was, "What the hay!"

Yes, I did take the Bucky on a three-day holiday to a working farm near Harlem, Georgia, not far from Augusta, birthplace of comedy film legend Oliver Hardy. Harlem, that is.

And, as any kitty caretaker will advise, setting a kitty loose on a farm field is risky business. They lose their way easily. And, once they discover all the farm smells, they pretend they don't know you.

Chief among pleasant agra-aromas is hay. Yes. Hay.

According to University of Fife professor Nicholas Fescue, catnip is an herb, not unlike mint. Hay is mostly grass, occasionally mixed with barley, wheat, Cheerios and Cap'n Crunch – most of which are not highly recommended for human consumption – whereas catnip may be delightfully dunked in steaming water for a pleasant afternoon tea or aerial-sprayed from low-flying aircraft to calm civilians protesting the increased cost of video streaming services.

Bucky discovered all of this on a warm and sunny Harlem July afternoon. My goodness she had fun. Prancing like a reindeer the day after Christmas, The Buckster cautiously circled one of those large rolled bales, drawing closer on each circumnavigation of the giant, until she felt it safe for her nose to touch the stuff.

"Whoa. What is this grand stinker?" she exclaimed. She wasn't intoxicated in the way she might with catnip but it was clear she was not moving her nose for an instant. For the casual observer, had this been winter, the scene might appear to be a cat with its nose or tongue stuck to a freezing tractor wheel.

Sniff the hay for ten minutes. Fall over on the field. Walk around the field like a drunken sailor. Sniff the hay for ten more minutes. This was a happy time. A lovely few days with Bucky in the summer warmth of Georgia at a time when it was possible for everyone enjoy a rural holiday with a catnip julip and vote.

And yes, when it was time to leave, she pranced excruciatingly slowly to her car carrier and entered without a fuss.

Bucky's Higher Education

It is of the utmost importance for cat companions and caregivers to recognize a cat's keen curiosity, the need to be doing something in those minutes when not napping. Failing to keep their minds engaged most certainly can lead them down that dark path to tail chasing.

As a teen, Bucky studied hard. Lessons included English, housekeeping, Christmas tree decorating, knitting and competitive soccer. A short period of tail chasing followed these educational challenges.

Bucky's Graduation Picture. Carnegie Mellon Structural Engineer Training.

During a brief residence in Pittsburgh, once referred to as "The West" in the MGM Cinerama movie *How the West Was Won*,

Bucky took evening courses at Carnegie Mellon University: Courses in structural engineering with a concentration in bird feeders. She passed all her course work with honors but actual on-the-job work was found to have too many distractions.

Tail-Chasing is Humiliating

I know it's back there and it's just a matter of time before I bite it!

"Gonna get that tail!
Once and for all! Gonna get it!"

As mentioned just a few lines back if you were paying attention, Bucky seldom chased her tail. The tail is a pesky thing. Two in the morning and your kitty is whirling around in a circle fast enough to make even the most cruise-seasoned, seaworthy cat parent a little dizzy. Yup. She's chasing after that pesky tail again. Seems that poor tail is always at risk. But "why" is the question we want answered. Why this odd behavior? Just as perplexed are animal behaviorists worldwide and cats themselves.

A 2021 study by graduate students at the International University of Feline Studies in Glasgow, Scotland, is revealing in that it was the first-time cats themselves were asked this critical question.

Some typical responses:

International	University of Feline Studies - Glasgow
	Why cats chase tails – 2021 study
6 mo -1 yr	Woke up one morning and there it was.
1 yr – 3 yr	Suppose you had some thing dangling from your body.
3 yr – 5 yr	What tail?
5 yr – 10 yr	It's not a tail; it's a portable modesty panel.
10 yr – 20 yr	It's none of your business.

Leading the research group was Professor Lars Little, PhD, who has studied feline behavior for sixty-two years.

PJR: Dr. Little, when did you first become interested in animal behavior?

LL: Fact is, everyone observes animals but most do not study them. They are content with the joy animals bring them.

PJR: But there must have been a special moment in time when you recognized animals were different from people, though many people do have fur an act aggressively especially after a few beers and national elections.

LL: Born to a circus family as I was, being carried by the scrub of my neck to dine at a mother lion's dairy is a memory I still hold dear. That's probably where it all started.

PJR: Professor Little, our story here is about tail chasing. What was your earliest such experience?

LL: I was thirteen years old and would sometimes find it floundering around and making my pants sorta tent-out watching Marilyn Monroe movies.

PJR: I see. Are we talking about the same thing here?

LL: Oh yes.

PJR: Well then.

Of course I see it. Right there.
Looking like it's part of the window
or plant or something.
I'll get it!

Bucky hardly ever chased her tail. But like many kitty caregivers and companions, I wondered if this is normal behavior. The consensus is that it is for some.

Kittens, it is believed, are simply exploring themselves just as any human child might.

"Look, I've got eyebrows. I've got five wiggly thingies on end of my hand." Perfectly normal.

They may even see their tail as a kind of chase toy wherein they are always just a few furry hairs ahead of the silly thing. Even for adult cats, the tail is a toy ready, willing and able to break the day's boredom.

Experienced cat partners understand the infatuation with things that move, especially things that move unexpectedly. That's why we play "catch-my-finger-if-you-can" games with the sweeties. Why they love to pounce on a bug. However, Bucky once confided that she could no longer do anything so humiliating.

The last time I saw her chasing her tail she was just two years old. I held the end of it in my hand. HRB turned. Stared at me and said, "Who said you could play this game!"

I'm not a doctor, though I have written about doctors in soap operas and spoken with actors who play doctors on television and in the movies. From what they have told me, tail chasing should be considered normal until adulthood. Then, you should stop chasing your tail and your cat will likely do the same. If tail chasing continues into adulthood, a vet's professional advice could be considered.

Thinking Inside the Box

Look. I'm Invisable.

The iconic kitty image. Not cat in the hat, Dr. Zeus. * Cat in the box.

I really relate to some of the theories about why cats love to hop into boxes. Why they sometimes fight their way in and then just sit there looking, ... well, shall we say, silly.

One such notion – not an actual theory yet – is that our kitties, Bucky explained, often prefer to hide from reality, looking for a special, quiet, low-visibility, sound- and sight- insulated environment where they can escape the stress of their day – stress caused by innumerable unsolved problems. Chief among them:

- Where am I?

- Why am I here?

- Why does Trump still believe he won re-election?

- Why did I slide into a bathtub filled with water?

- Why do people care so much about upholstery?

- Why don't I tire of eating food from a bowl on the floor?

- Why does my tail continue to believe it needs to follow me everywhere? Get a life of your own.

- Why are flies allowed to go anywhere they want and sit on birthday cakes, whereas I catch hell?

Bucky believed all these questions caused her stress. And without access to appropriate pharmaceuticals from nearby school playgrounds, coping sometimes, she said, became difficult.

Over millennia, ** cats have come to recognize that small spaces, inaccessible to humans, have proved safe havens***. In fact, Bucky's Danbury, Connecticut****, vet, Dr. Hans Pawbrite, had built a wall in his waiting room with cubby hole boxes where our superior kitties could sit and await their appointment surrounded on five sides by airport lounge-grade carpeting, safe in the knowledge that nothing can "get them" from the back, top, bottom, sides except maybe Vanna White, then co-host of the incredibly popular *Wheel of Fortune* TV show.

Information provided by the Purina company cites a study conducted by the University of Utrecht***** recently discovered another reason why cats love boxes. The study was performed on a group of shelter cats, and around half were assigned boxes and the other half were not. "The research discovered that the cats with the boxes actually recovered faster and adapted to their environment quicker. This shows that boxes are incredibly beneficial for cats to help deal with change!" Buy Purina. And a box.

Cardboard boxes are good insulators. Carboard was an amazing World War Two scientific discovery. A war hero, really.

Prior to cardboard, there was only the paper bag, common to 1940s supermarket checkouts. Great for carrying groceries: strong, manufactured from sustainable sources and easily recyclable into more paper bags. Their only flaw, pointed out by the National Institute of Plastics Producers Lobbying Everywhere

(NIPPLE), was that paper bags were inexpensive, Earth friendly and would generally have been approved by Jesus.

I would often carry Bucky around the house in a supermarket paper bag.

Bottom line, says Bucky, we believe that in a box we are invisible.

---

*   Dr. Zeus spelled backwards is Dr. Suez.

**   Not related to Trump's former wife.

***   Not related to Richie Havens whose 2005 hit LP compilation *High Flyin' Bird* offended many a feline.

**** Connecticut's correct abbreviation is Conn. Not CT instituted by the U.S. Postal Service under pressure from IBM, an Alabama Senator and other computer giants in an effort to save money on toner cartridges.

This silly cartoon is placed here for many reasons:

- Instructional value
- Comic relief
- Page filler

The publisher believes it's been successful on all counts. Your comments are welcome at HRBBuckshot7@gmail.com.

Toads – If it moves, it's mine!

Bucky, like most indoor cats, did enjoy the occasional romp on real grass, not that tacky indoor-outdoor carpeting found at miniature golf courses.

I was never concerned about her getting lost or into some sort puddy danger because she was only allowed out with me close by keeping watch. Besides, smart kitty as she was, Bucky would only trample areas she had seen and was familiar with from her living room perch.

What's to discover, you ask? Everything. So many things that look like catnip. A small puddy puddle of rain water where bugs were a favorite. Top of the top-ten list of likes: frogs, toads, princes in disguise.

The Buckster preferred toads.

Backyard Toad Alert!

What about frogs, you say?   What about tadpoles? Frogs and toads are both amphibians, meaning they both have wheels and floats. They look similar.

Toads are primarily landlubbers with thicker skin, often brownish, while frogs tend to be more greenish and have very large eyes in order to better see approaching Buckys. Both begin life, as many of us do, as an egg that develops into a tadpole – not a toadpole, a reasonably ugly-looking thing that spends much of its early tadpoley life in water where Bucky-like creatures sometimes find them in little pools of garden rain water where they can be stared at and played with endlessly before meeting their end as a discarded biological unit to be discovered somewhere near a garage downspout (eavestrough) days later by puddy's caretaker.

Now a Word from a Sponsor – Plastic Cat Toys

Crap from China (CFC) kitty toys bound to meet with distain and stains on your carpet or keyboard.

If you find the above-mentioned live biological toys idea way too gross for consideration as décor or entertainment appointments for your home, you are more likely to consider stuffed things and plastic – what kitty lovers term CFC (Crap from China). We say this, not in an uncaring way that could possibly injure the feelings of little plastic molecules and their lawyers because I feel their pain and anguish as one of my most valued possessions is eighty-five percent plastic. I refer here, of course, to my 2010 Honda Civic.

Face it: Store-bought kitty toys are to a cat what a button-down dress shirt is to an eight-year-old boy on Christmas morning. Or to an eight-year-old girl handed a beautifully-wrapped-and-tied-with-a-pretty-red-Christmassy-ribbon copy of *A Girl's First Thesaurus*.

Visit the toy section of your local pet store or Wal-Mart-Atorium and inhale. Take a deep breath. What you are smelling is the aroma of plastic molecules lightly sprayed with Chanel No. 109, Mist-o-Feline, manufactured in the Alabama region of China.

Don't insult your kitty. He/she will drop a hairball on your pillow in retaliation.

You ask, "Are there any manufactured toys acceptable to cats?" Of course. (See image below somewhere near the following punctuation mark.)

BUCKY-APPROVED (BA) MANUFACTURED TOYS.

Just Ring the Bloomin' Doorbell

For millennia, * cats needed to rely on a human's willingness and patience in opening the door for outside strolls and bodily functions. You know the routine: a light pawing of the door and sweet meow and the door opens. Once outside, and within forty seconds, a light pawing of the door and sweet meow, and the door once again opens and the little sweetie walks in. This is followed by a repeat of the routine at least twelve times, enduring the human's "What is it? In or Out!" Just plain annoying for kitties.

Bucky, with a genuine *Popular Mechanics* certificate in home electrical devices, has raised the "What is it? In or out?" discussion to new heights.

Rather than energy-wasting meows and door-pawing, The Buckster has taught herself how to use the doorbell. Heavens to Tom and Jerry, you say, that could be annoying. Sufferin' succotash, Tweety Bird!

Now, it's ring, ring and Bucky saying, "Would you like to buy life insurance?" Again. Again. Again.

Catpeople

No. It's not two words. It's *catpeople**. One word.

A person who cares for, loves, adores, cherishes cats is a *cat person*.

A *catpeople* is a creature that really is biologically part cat. Not just a human that humiliatingly meows at their cat and thinks it's adorable.

Illustrating this important point, Bucky provided a movie poster that for years she had been sitting on.

The 1982 movie *Cat People* starred the amazingly beautiful and sterling and studied actress Nastassja Kinski (pronounced *kin-ski.* And, yes, her first name is spelled correctly). Bucky explained that the producer, RKO Pictures (of 1932 *King Kong* fame and only crap 3-D movies after that; but *Citizen* Kane wasn't that bad) had originally titled the film correctly as *Catpeople.* Kinski, a catpeople herself insisted on accuracy including the correct spelling. Children with master's degrees in screenwriting, however, insisted *Catpeople* was just plain wrong and that audiences who could spell, though few, "would become painfully infuriated, not unlike an ingrown townail (sic)," they wrote in a widely-distributed secret memo written on actual paper.

So, it came to be. *Cat People.* It was a big box office hit.

Nastassja Kinski was well-received in the film. She and her kind loved it. "Of course, she was," The Buckster said. "She wasn't acting; she was just being herself."

We'd like to show you a picture here of at least the *Cat People*** movie poster with Nastassja (pronounced *bu-tee-ful*), but copyright laws prohibit this except for little, tinny images that are difficult to reproduce but permitted under copyright laws of many left-wing civilized countries such as Sweden, provided they illustrate an important educational point.

So, here it is.

(Very tiny picture RKO lawyers will not be offended by because this caption is bigger than the photo.)

But the important educational point Bucky wished to make is that there are times when humans will go to extremes to befriend, or simply get on the right side of a cat.

One seriously failed example, from Ulcer, Texas, a community of 870 sour-pussed people, shows sisters, identical twins, Wanda and Wandaloose Glimpse, donning hideously-fake kitty whiskers in an ill-fated attempt to befriend a kitty and get the sweetie to swallow a pill.

"Do they seriously think we buy into this?" Bucky told an assembled reporter at the National Press Club in Washington.

Wanda and Wandaloose Glimpse have long-since apologized for the idiocy of their maybe-well-intentioned but ill-conceived plan and were granted mercy at the Pettown Court of Appeals, sentenced to 60 days community service at the animal shelter.

* *Catpeople,* whether referring to a single person or more than one person, is always written and referred to as *Catpeople.*   There is no singular or plural.

** It is widely believed that RKO Pictures and their lawyers should not leap for joy at possibly finding a legal copyright infringement case here because Bucky has low friends in high places and is just a sweetie of a cat children love and trying to tell a story.

A Brush with Nature

Brushing our teeth is something we understand as necessary. We do it at least three times a day – more when we are dating. That's possibly 1,095 routine brushes annually; 2,187 brushes if dating. But what about your kitty companion? Isn't oral hygiene just as necessary for the puddy in your life?

Before Bucky began sharing her life with me, I never thought about feline dental hygiene.

"Peter, animals get into serious trouble if their teeth and gums are not kept clean and healthy," Jessica, my stunning and professional personal dental hygienist told me.

Mouth stuffed with cotton, plastic saliva vacuum tubes and an array of potentially injury-causing sharp metal objects, I nodded and replied, "UAkerjhrkmabgg!" That's patient dental talk for, "I cannot form actual words with all these Inquisition era objects in my mouth, but I totally agree with you, Jessica. May I rinse now?"

HRB Buckshot standing at the bathroom sink with a brush in her paw is how I imagined it was done. Really. I had no clue whatsoever. *

Naturally, I understood that I needed to further study the issue, discovering that cats, like many superior creatures, use natural products found all around them for this purpose.   In the wild, meaning the backyard, kitties nibble on grass or herbs, for example, chewing as best they can before puking it on your living room carpet. The theory is that the chewing of natural thingies triggers enzymes in saliva, aiding the release of tooth tartar that finds its way out of the body one way or another.   But it's a slow process and teeth problems will develop over time.

I began to realize that Bucky might have tooth decay problems when it was apparent that her breath smelled remarkably like my own.

I asked whether she had been brushing regularly, perhaps late at night. This line of questioning led nowhere, and so, I decided to take matters into my own hands

A word of caution here. Not every kitty likes human fingers in their mouth and some, especially older cats, will help you understand their feelings by biting you

* You'll note that "whatsoever" is actually the melding of three important English language words: "what", "so" and "ever." Teenagers further condensed or abbreviated or contracted this cumbersome tripartite word into the simpler and more useful common usage of today's parenting: "whatever."

Yes, The Buckster bit me, but ever so gently, a love bite really. Afterall, despite her GED and advanced degree in structural engineering, hissing, meows, biting, a few words of English and poop and pee are pretty much her major forms of communication.

OK. So, the tooth brush was out and I tried again with just my finger and some dental cream from my nearby pet palace.

You are correct. That did not work.

Next, my finger and a very mild solution of peroxide. Very mild. Peroxide gets a bad rap because it was long-associated with bleaching hair blonde, useful in Hollywood and high schools in the 1950s. Mainly girls used it. But peroxide is an important disinfectant as well – used to clean wounds. Peroxide (actually hydrogen peroxide, if you want to be accurate), like "whatsoever" is the melding of three important words: "hydrogen", "per" and "oxide." Any school child knows hydrogen is powerful; that's why it's used to make bombs. Oxide means oxygen, a good thing when it's not making rust. We use oxygen in great quantities every day. We even make water with it. Many of our larger oceans and lakes contain these elements in a combination known as H_2O. However, when you take two atoms of hydrogen and two – not just one – atoms of oxygen and mix them in an ordinary kitchen blender, you get H_2O_2. Hydrogen Per Oxide.

Bucky tolerated this for several weeks, but I could still see some abscess developing.

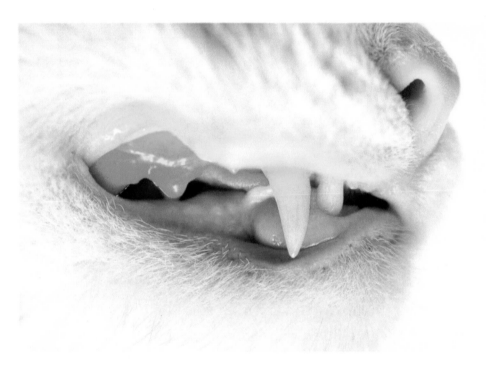

AREA OF ABSCESS ENHANCED FOR EDUCATIONAL PURPOSES.

Time to call travelling vet and radio talk show host Dr. Norah von Worthington, a super caregiver who comes to your home for a physical. Your cat's physical, not hers.

Using a pair of blue surgical gloves lightly rubbed with tuna can oil, Dr. Norah quickly arrived at the cause of the problem. Three teeth were badly abscessed and needed extraction, not a home procedure.

With very little fuss, Bucky remained in Dr. Norah's arms while we poured her into a car carrier. Bucky, that is, not Dr. Norah.

Off they went to the vet clinic. The extraction went smoothly and Bucky made a full and painless recovery in just two days.

CAUTION. Dr. Norah strongly advises against putting unapproved or non-prescribed foreign substances in your sweet kitty's mouth even if you see commercials on TV promoting such things.

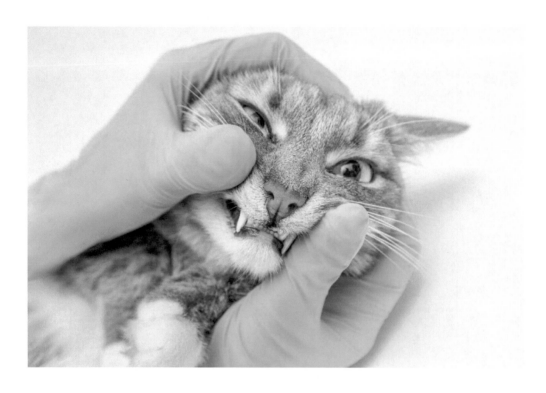

The next week, Bucky spent much of her time sitting atop a bedroom door.

(CC BY-SA 2.0) OhLizz @ Flickr

Clairvoyance Club

As reported in the earliest edition of WikiCatOfFactsAnd Theories.com (WCOFAT), Bucky was the founder and CEO (Cat Empress Official) of Bucky's Clairvoyance Club (membership: two), headquartered in Danbury, Connecticut.

It all started quite by accident, Bucky told a gathered reporter from *Litterature Weekly Magazine*.

In the summer of 1982, Bucky began experiencing frequent and unusual head-shaking episodes. Short-lasting but troubling. There appeared no pain or other symptoms beyond an uncanny (meaning *without can*) and casual tap on some object, often a book.

Bucky and I marched to Dr. Needleman, our local vet, who explored the puddy from nose to tail but could find only hair, a condition normal for a cat. Needleman peered into Bucky's eyes. A steady person-to-cat moment.

"Have you considered getting Bucky a crystal ball?" Needleman asked with a seriousness mostly reserved for atomic scientists at cocktail hour. *

"I believe your Buckshot may have super cat powers and able to read into the future," Needleman said with the utmost pre-cocktail hour seriousness. "Trust me on this. Was I wrong about switching to Science Diet?"

* To learn more about the jovial scientists who helped build various nuclear bombs, you may wish to get a copy of *Surely, You're Joking, Mr. Feynman* by Richard A. Feynman. It's a laugh-a-minute account of exploding things in the New Mexico desert.

"You little devil you," I said to The Buckster with a determination in my voice and stare from my eyes that meant only that we could make some money from this discovery to cover our aging years on a farm somewhere near a Papa John's Pizza Joint (PJPJ).

The two of us packed ourselves in to the 1980 Honda Civic and headed downtown Danbury, sight of more than a few UFO sightings, locating first the local PJPJ where we bought two slices with mushrooms. In a small back-of-shop booth, I ate all of mine while The Buckster merely licked the toppings from hers.

Next, WalMart before it became Wal-Mart – or was it the other way around? It was filled with Arkansas-designed stuff manufactured in one of the more miserable provinces of China, thus taking millions of jobs from totally unskilled U.S. labor plastic crap makers.

A WalMart associate directed us to aisle 217 where we found tennis balls.

It was Bucky, clearly using her special gift, who suggested we go directly to the source.

Brilliant. Why didn't I think of this?

On the northeast side of town, the Civic, under HRB's direction, pulled into what appeared to be a long-abandoned strip mall where a scantily-clad person of the female persuasion greeted our arrival and motioned to roll down the window for a free coupon of some sort entitling us to "The Special."

"Do you know where we can find crystal balls," I asked.

"Wrong thing to ask," Bucky squealed from the back seat.

Nose and paw to the side window, HRB clearly pointed to an antique shop aptly named "Now Antiques – Treasures of Past and Present. $1 and Up". Our six feet ventured in.

"Geeeeeze, this place is dusty," Bucky spouted with a kitty sneeze. "Will this story be dragging on much longer?"

An old woman with a giant wart on her nose the size of a Grimm fairy tale welcomed us.

"You two just dropping in for my dinner?"

Bucky took a few pads in reverse.

"We're looking for a used but serviceable crystal ball for the kitty here."

"Might have such a thing, maybe. Does the kitty here want some extra paws to go with it? Rabbit, perhaps?"

Bucky glanced over her shoulder ready to sprint to the door.

"So, just occult-curious are we. I have just the thing."

And with that, Grizelda retreated backwards to the back room. Before we could say "EXIT" or "911", the lovely Grizelda reappeared holding the treasure. Bucky and I gasped. It was a genuine Captain Midnight Ovaltine Crystal Ball.

"$27 cash for you, two-feet. Special $8.95 for the kitty, she seems a perfect specimen."

Bucky reached into her purse and counted out $9.00. "Keep the change," she offered.

As the Danbury evening sun, not to be confused with the weekly newspaper of the same name, settled and shadows became longer, we set up the crystal that Bucky decided to call Crystal.

A misty smoke began to appear in the globe.

It's working.

"Looks like it's just smoke or TV static," Bucky observed. "Maybe we need an antenna."

"I think it just needs to warm up."

"What is this, 1951?"

"You're the mystic cat. Say something. Use your powers!"

"I can't. I'm having trouble following who is saying what here," Bucky said. "OK. Sim Sala Bim."

"What does that mean, Bucky?"

"I have no idea. I heard it on a David Copperfield show."

And then, the cloud of smoke cleared. There it was, October 9, 1982. Bucky had long predicted a musical based on the T.S. Eliot 1939 book, *Old Possum's Book of Practical Cats*. Her crystal confirmed it all.

"My Ovaltine Crystal Ball works. See, I am clairvoyant because the crystal confirmed my prediction."

On closer inspection, the newspaper front page was not telling of a future opening on Broadway but one already two days past. *CATS* opened October 7, 1982. We turned and looked at each other, puzzled. Then back to the crystal. It changed its glass globe image, now reading "Drink Ovomaltine", the European version of Ovaltine. "Please deposit 25 francs."

Bucky and I realized the crystal had not lived up to our expectations and cut deeply into her nap time.

DOS – macOS – WINDOWS - LINUX – APPLE iOS - BOS -

A computer is just a bread box with wires and useless warranties without an Operating System, the OS. Think crumbs here. Thankfully, history has provided our bread boxes with something called an "operating system." People such as Bill Gates, using one small example with glasses, is arguably* the creator, inventor, developer of the first somewhat workable operating system. It was called DOS, meaning Doesn't Operate Satisfactorily. For the first time, all those bread boxes we bought at Radio Shack** and other computer-savvy retailers could be easily upgraded to a condition known in technical circles as "working." Since that memorable DOS moment in 1892 (not a typo), at least nine other computer operating systems have been introduced in the ever-ongoing challenge to make our daily lives more productive and enjoyable. Kitty caregivers fully understand this.

Kitty caregivers also know their cat's curiosity will eventually find your computer.

---

*   *Arguably* means it may not be true, but we are allowed to argue about it.

**   Radio Shack was a wonderful place to buy all kinds of starter electronics, TVs, radios, turntables, plastic toys and Young Sheldon's first computer.

I purchased my first personal computer in 1981, a magnificent Commodore 64. Early computer experts often referred to this wonderful machine as the "Commode-A-Door." It was an amazing piece of plastic with everything one needed already built in. Don't equate that "64" with any computer term currently in use. I think it referred to the number of keys on the keyboard if you owned two keyboards.

The Commodore 64 was a pre-Bucky model. My first genuine business-like personal computer was a Compaq. A great machine that arrived with many wires and plugs. It worked. And this was Bucky's first unit and she quickly applied her curiosity to the task of making it more kitty friendly.

The first things Bucky's keen vision and extraordinary hearing capabilities noticed: The keyboard was a beige-ish color and the keys made a clicking sound like an old typewriter. Beige, we all know, is bland and cats are anything but bland. Next, clicking old typewriter-key sounds are very annoying to cats, Bucky explained. Gives cats guilt feelings as it causes them to mistakenly believe something is happening – an activity, perhaps – while they are trying to nap.

The first weekend in the Compaq's new home, Bucky solved both problems

A transparency note here: The furball or hairball pictured above was from a light day and used merely as a less gross illustration. Had we wished to be totally accurate, we'd show you the picture that follows which is more like that the average kitty caregiver can expect on reporting to work in the morning. But, of course, the photo is way too gross, so try to put the image out of your mind.

Arguably (You'll remember the footnote on this from a previous page.), hairballs are gross, but look at them differently for a moment. Kitties, though superior creatures, do have certain limitations when it comes to communication. These are limited to:

1. Meows
2. Hisses
3. Poops
4. Pees
5. Bites

6. Hairballs
7. Upholstery cleaning
8. Biting your nose
9. Thumbing its nose at your poor excuse for its dinner
10. Sitting in the bathroom sink sipping water

The hairball, though, is very nearly the perfect problem solver. It comes forward late at night while you are trying to sleep. It's ugly, messy. Did we mention gross.

So, heaving a hairball on my computer keyboard was the perfect solution to a problem I did not have. Anticipating a recurrence of this action, I bought three new keyboards. Bucky took note.

For a moment now, and just to present another side of the issue, suppose you were unable to speak the language of your caregiver and had just eaten a delicious meal of salmon while having your hair cut. Well, you get the point.

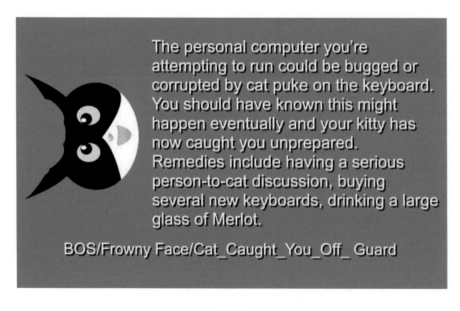

The personal computer you're attempting to run could be bugged or corrupted by cat puke on the keyboard. You should have known this might happen eventually and your kitty has now caught you unprepared. Remedies include having a serious person-to-cat discussion, buying several new keyboards, drinking a large glass of Merlot.

BOS/Frowny Face/Cat_Caught_You_Off_ Guard

As you can now understand, the BOS, the Bucky Operating System, is the feline version of an unwanted Microsoft Plugin or Plug and Play. It gets into the system without your knowing, without your permission and causes ERROR 499/BOS/Frowny Face/Cat_Caught_You_Off_Guard.

More contemporary computer instructions are similar to the one pictured nearby, wherein, users are placed at the very end of the schematic giving fair warning.

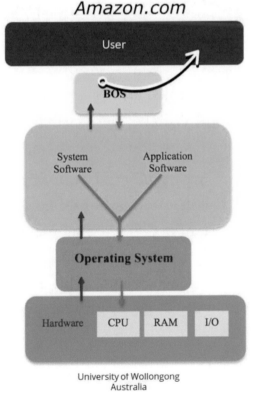

BOS -The Bucky Computer
Operating System Explained
in *The Book of Bucky, now at*
Amazon.com

University of Wollongong
Australia

Pharaoh Faucet

Because Bucky confided in me and shared the history of faucet sipping questions. With her permission, I can now share the answers with my fellow cat persons.

First, if we were to carefully track our kitty treks to the litter box each day, we'd discover that kitties do not like peeping Toms during these all-important and private moments of relief. But, if we did peep - not saying I have, we'd come to the realization that cats do not drink very much water. This also explains, Bucky revealed, the reason their water bowls never seem to empty. This is an actual fact.

You may have forgotten, while still others never knew, that cats are desert creatures. They first came to Earth in saucer-shaped ships from an as yet unknown world outside our solar system, landing first in North Africa, in the land that would become modern day Egypt. Egypt is a dry land, most notably because of a lack of water. Not a problem for the visitors as they were and continue to be obligate carnivores, meaning they will never share your interest in vegetables and things with roots in dirt. They eat meat because, among other things, meat has high water content.

The point here is that cats, ordinarily, have a low thirst level. Most of their moisture comes from food. Problem is, for some kitties, the low moisture content of dry food really gets them annoyed.

Egypt, we remember from those odd times we were awake in grade school history class, was ruled by a weird family of bird-like people who called themselves "pharaohs", meaning odd looking humans with long beaks made of pure gold, descendant from Elizabeth Taylor.

Most "pharaohs" said they were gods. People who worked mostly hauling large rocks to various places, believed the pharaohs and worshipped them. The pharaohs loved the newcomers because they were so cute and possessed knowledge of the stars. The earliest known pharaoh to recognize the foreign visitors as equals was His Majesty, Pharaoh Iso Sceles who is remembered to this day for his early work on triangles, the basis of all pyramids and at least one musical instrument.

While Bucky's roots can accurately be traced only to about the year 800, all cats are direct descendants of those early pioneers

113

landing in Egypt some ten-thousand years ago, during the early days when television was still black & white.

It was Bucky's early ancestors who showed pharaohs how to survive in a dry climate. They explained to the high royals that water was a principal ingredient in beer, and as the Egyptians were already growing grains such as wheat, Bucky's ancestors showed Ms. Taylor and her various Italian husbands living in Egypt, how to grow barley to mix with some Nile River water to make a beverage that would sustain them until the British invaded and colonised, making Egypt the grand land it is today with warm beer. *

Oh. Right. Sipping water from faucets. If cats are unable get enough water from their meat meal (MM), they would wander down to the Nile and sip from the running river because they knew the water upstream had not been peed in by lower orders of animals such as people and goats. To boot, cats knew it was safer to sip water out in the open than from a bowl where predictors might find them. In short, running water, even the sound of running water, simply was better. That is now hard-wired into all kitties, large and small. So, what chance does our degrading, humiliating plastic or metal bowl on the floor have?

What can you do about this?

NOTHING!!!!!! It is the natural order of things. Never tamper with the natural order of things.

As for Bucky, she told me to keep the bathtub tap open just slightly for a refreshing sip of running Nile water when it pleased her and at those times when it would most annoy me.

Interesting Factoid: History now recognizes His Majesty, Pharaoh Iso Sceles, as inventor of the world's very first beer cooler, pictured here.

ACTUAL SIZE: 55 BY 35 INCHES

The Aero

It was 1987 or 1990 when Bucky and I traveled by car from Connecticut to Hollywood for her important work on stereo sound at Dolby Labs. The work went well. She met an array of celebrities. Occupied the Star Suite at a nearby Earthquake and Forest Fire Motel. But, no question. When the work was at an end, Her Royalness wanted to get home ASAP. This involved visiting a bevy of Southern California used car lots, of which, there are just three, to sell the Honda and buy airline tickets. Californians would never want to be seen driving a used vehicle of any kind. And this was a 1980 or '81 Honda Civic LAers believed should be allowed to rust out in peace in an abandoned farm yard. But there was more.

Salmo quæ incedunt quadrupedia, et usque in sempiternum

By appointment only
Buckyness Palace
HRBBuckshot7@gmail.com

Dear Loyal Subject,

We wish to express our royal displeasure with your choice of return transport from Hollywood.

Though mightily pleased with the opportunity to work with Dolby Labs on improvements to theatre and home stereo sound and for the lovely travel to La La Land by motor, the return trip was quite something of a disappointment.

You know we do not appreciate travel by aero.

The clouds were pretty, as was the flight crew. However, there simply was too much noise. If I wanted to hear babies crying, I'd have one of my own. My seatback table was an insult, we don't know why people tolerate it. The inflight tuna was tasteless. Walking down the aisle to our private litter loo was a serious challenge and we have the sore paws to prove it.

While we appreciate your having to sell your old Honda Civic to get me home more quickly, we advise that this never happen again.

Your sovereign has spoken.

Sigh.

The Unlikely Space Aero Hero

As you recently learned, had you been attentive, Bucky was not a fan of air travel, the *aero*, as she put it. And who could blame her. Air travel today makes a crowded Tokyo subway look like nirvana on a slow day. A hairball/furball on a computer keyboard would be a mild reaction to the thought of leaving the ground, despite the fact that her great ancestors arrived from somewhere well beyond our flawed, relatively round planet.

With this in mind, Bucky, like all superior and curious kitties, applied for a training program for kitties with a minimum of a GED for a possible space adventure.

"What could possibly go wrong? It's just an up and a down, right? I could be an internationally-revered celebrity," HRB, light-pawed, meowing hopefully.

By now, you must have recognized this extraordinary puddy's craving for learning and mild adventure outside well-recognized nap times.

Bucky responded to the following advertisement in the international and well-respected *Aerial Hairballs Unlimited Annual*, a Bucky magazine subscription for at least eight years.

So, there it was. Despite aversion to anything involving air, except for breathing purposes, Bucky responded to the advert and received an invitation to try out for the part. It just had to be cat ego. She simply wanted affirmation that her royalty was not a misplaced alternate fact.

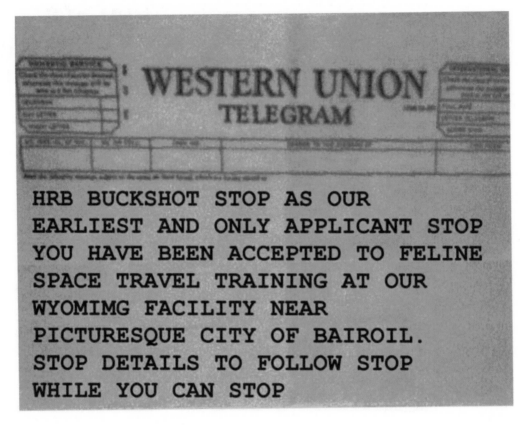

WESTERN UNION
TELEGRAM

HRB BUCKSHOT STOP AS OUR
EARLIEST AND ONLY APPLICANT STOP
YOU HAVE BEEN ACCEPTED TO FELINE
SPACE TRAVEL TRAINING AT OUR
WYOMIMG FACILITY NEAR
PICTURESQUE CITY OF BAIROIL.
STOP DETAILS TO FOLLOW STOP
WHILE YOU CAN STOP

No one knows the correct spelling of this Wyoming city nestled in the foothills of the ApalachaCola foothills. Bareoil, Bareall, Bearoil. This, despite Rudy Restivo, a possible relation not tested in a court of law, having been the sheriff of Laramie County, Wyoming, boasting an elevation of 9 feet, at some time in the not-so-distant-past.

I suggested that Bucky not jump into something she may have to jump out of. As for celeb status, she already had that. She insisted. So, I arranged an actual phone call with Cats in Space Ltd CEO Belinda Versace who explained some of the rigorous tasks Bucky would have to perform. These included:

1. Go up in a rocket leaving the Earth at approximately seven million miles per hour.

2. Return to Earth at a leisurely pace with a magnificent, silky view of the approaching ground at a location that might be unpredictable – perhaps Italy. She Twittered an illustration showing just how that might be achieved.

The lovely Belinda, best known as author of the wildly successful *Halloween is No Time for Cats*, recognizing some reticence in Bucky's voice offered to send actual flight simulator software and a rental spacesuit to Connecticut.

"Hey. An opportunity like this doesn't just fall into your lap everyday," Bucky explained.

"Thank goodness," I responded.

Six days later, UPS delivered everything Bucky needed, already assembled.

We tried it out.

I believe Alexander Graham Lindbergh put it best, "Any flight you can walk away from with only soiling your pants is a good one."

Up the Down Staircase

It's a well-known fact that kitties enjoy a post-midnight romp (PMR). It's a time when they can explore their home without the annoying meddling of a human constantly asking, "What are you doing?"

It was not long after a move into a lovely Danbury, Connecticut, townhouse with fireplaces in both living room and master bedroom, that the late-night action began.

12:09 AM, Friday, November 1, it was. Trick or treaters all nestled in their warm comfy beds with stomach aches from way too much junk candy. I, too, was appropriately nestled in my second-floor bedroom, blanket nicely tucked, eyes closed, sleep having just caught up with me.

SNAP. What sound is that?

LIGHT THUMPING. What sound is that? Why am I repeating myself?

SNAP. There it is again, I said again.

LIGHT THUMPING.

Now, I'm worried. Concerned an intruder has intruded, as RADAR on M*A*S*H might have said. The sounds continue. Beneath my bedroom door, that little space between the door bottom and the carpet. There it is. I can see the hallway staircase light switching on and off. The soft thumps. What midnight burglar would act in this manner. It's a sure giveaway to the vigilant Danbury Police patrolling that something is afoot.

I can't hide under the bed; that's where my Lionel train set rests on a plywood board so that I can play with it on those too-often lonely Friday nights. Best thing to do is to pad to the bedroom door. Quietly open it just a smidge, praying the hinge is a quiet one.

So far. So good. No need for a snack just yet.

The door is cracked open just the width of an eyeball.

The intruder! Right there. A *she*! A *she* intruder. A tabby *she* intruder.

Her Royalness was at the top of the staircase, staring up at the light switch. One of those three-way deals. She jumps up. Slaps the switch with a forceful right paw to the switchplate. Strikes the switch. The light goes off. Down the stairs she pads. Cats, you know, pad very well; it comes quite naturally to them. Down below, near the foot or pad of the staircase, Bucky pauses. Looks up at the bottom staircase three-way switch. Jump. Slaps the switchplate. The light goes on. From the eye-size crack in my bedroom door, I watch this creature repeat this little exercise several times before quietly padding (such a cute word) to the staircase upper landing outside my door. Again, she arrives prepared to strike the switch. She sees me standing there, hands in my robe pockets. Ever so innocently, Bucky turns her head and looks up at me, smiling. I know she is smiling.

"Just checking the electrical system. It's all okay. You can go back to bed," Bucky says as she nonchalantly saunters to the bedroom, jumps up and curls up on my pillow. Her night's work now complete.

Stately Anvil Manor

There was a brief period in my life when I was creatively and financially successful. It didn't last very long. But while it did, life was grander than those gray, snow-filled days in Danbury tending the fireplace. We, Bucky and I, lived in London. That place in England where Judy Dench lives and from where or whence Bucky traces her family at least to the first century and Alfred the Great's kitty, Alfred the Lesser.

Bucky travels most places with me, provided it's not by motor. By aero is fine, particularly when we fly First Class.

The reason for the pond crossing was research and screenplay writing for a British-funded sequel to the successful 1963 biographical movie, *PT 109*, about U.S. Navy Lieutenant John Kennedy's heroic World War II achievements in the Pacific as commanding officer of a PT boat (motor torpedo boat) sinking under enemy fire. His true-life story is that of a genuine hero and man dedicated to his crew.

That was a wonderful movie, that *PT-109*. I screened it many times with Bucky in what the Brits term a "reception room" at Stately Anvil Manor (SAM), outside London and near the famous Ealing Studios where such great TV shows as *Downton Abbey* were produced.

As a kitty, Bucky's water and water-like interests are limited, except for drinking from the Nile River or a bathroom tap. But she watched this water-related movie with great curiosity and a certain mystical awareness.

Have you noticed how my language has changed to a faux BBC-like style since being in England. This is not a question, so no question mark is required. Do not make me explain why!

Stately Anvil Manor sat precariously on a slippery parcel leading down to a river fishing pier where even a raccoon would not express interest in any water-borne food substance.

By day, mostly rainy days, Stately Anvil Manor was quite interesting, if not Halloweenie in appearance. By night, it was positively eerie, not unlike the lake in New York State named for famed Lagastino Prize in Science winner, Dr. Timothy Eerie. The lake is one of the Great Lakes separating the United States from Canada, a war-like nation to the north.

As a Navy Public Affairs Officer during one of America's several misguided military adventures, I had exposure to so many sights, sounds, people, stories, secrets and certain STDs*. It was experience maybe only one-million other Navy types could claim and a certain asset in keeping this story on track.

But. this story was really Bucky's idea. As we know from a previous chapter, Bucky is modestly clairvoyant and she soon met and formed an arguably-odd relationship with Stately Anvil Manor's butler, Anvil.

BUCKY OBSERVES ANVIL MIXING A SECRET POTION.

Anvil, Bucky learned, was the sole beneficiary of the heirless Lord Warwick Castleberry, forty-ninth in the line of succession to the British Crown. And possessor of what many who knew him believed were relatively benign powers of medium-to-strong spiritualism and clairvoyancy, strengths, many, including myself, believe are possessed by HRB.

The original *PT–109* story dwelled far too long on soon-to-be-president of the United States Kennedy. My story, more properly, dwells far too long on the craft's mascot, an adult male cat named Ghost. While the PT-109 crew survived, Ghost was never found.

Studying a vintage photo of the real U.S. Navy PT-109, Anvil lightly coated the black & white image with the secret potion. The result was nothing short of astonishing.

ANVIL AND BUCKY DISCOVER AN IMAGE OF GHOST

Over the decades since the conclusion of the war, reports of sightings of an all-black cat with a slight reddish glow have been received by the U.S. Pacific Command.

Both Anvil and Bucky believe that the ghost of Ghost travels the Pacific islands in search of a way to get home to the Creator Cat in the sky.

That's how the movie *Ghost of PT-109* was born.

A STORY OF AMERICA'S LOVE FOR KITTIES DURING WARTIME

Further details will just have to wait until the movie comes to Netflix or a cable cooking show.

Thank you, Bucky and Anvil.

* STD. If you don't know what this is, you should Google it and not engage in lovemaking of any sort.

Spring Ahead. Fall Behind.

These four words – "Spring Ahead" and "Fall Behind", passed along since the earliest generations of life on Earth, have attained the importance time needs to be both meaningful and pleasurable.

As noted earlier, Bucky traces her family line back to Alfred the Lesser, circa 871. Please remember this; it will be on the final. But it is proven and widely known that all cats originated in ancient Egypt. While not known to Bucky, she has long-believed that Nephertutu, a goddess to the ancient world, was actually where her family line on Earth began.

NEPHERTUTU – CIRCA 3500 BCE

Nephertutu,'s status is confirmed by the fact that the ancients created magnificent statues of their goddesses from valuable materials such as quartzite, diorite, marmite, granite, basalt and copper alloys and buoys.

It was during this time that time was first noticed. Ancient world Egyptian moms, for example, would see their children off to school and ask, "What time will you be home?" The kids didn't know. Fathers, busy at pyramid construction sites, were told by union bosses to be certain to take time for lunch. But no one knew what time that was. Even pharaohs became upset with this *time* situation and threatened that unless someone figured this *time* thing, no one would be buried alive in pointy royal tombs.

This led Nephertutu to study the problem and develop a sand-powered device she called a "clock", named for the royal household kitty goddess caretaker, Mrs. Rancid Clock, who would never show up for work at the correct time.

While a beautiful work of art and design, this first Nephertutu clock failed to catch on because, it was pointed out, Roman numerals, the standard for elegance, would not be invented for another two-thousand years. Moreover, the first clock had a copper mechanism that needed to be wound regularly and a winding key would not be invented for a least another three-thousand years. Thus, the first clock became just another artifact, buried in the sands of time.

It wasn't long after, though, that goddess Nephertutu experimented with sand falling through a glass bubble as a source of power for winding clocks. This is how we get the all-too-common phrase used on many of today's television soap operas: "The Sands of Time."

RANCID CLOCK RECENTLY UNEARTHED BY ARCHEOLOGISTS

To this day, Bucky keeps a working model of the Nephertutu-inspired timepiece on a living room table where she can watch the sand trickle down creating the energy needed to wind her favorite clock. When all the sand in the upper bubble has moved to the lower, Bucky then knows she must turn over the glass device and take a well-timed nap.

Modern clocks utilize electric-powered motors rather than sand, but few are as accurate at the Nephertutu-inspired clocks of the ancient past, and none are consistently synchronized for the demands of Daylight Saving Time's Spring Ahead and Fall Behind.

MODERN CLOCKS SYNCHRONIZED FOR DAYLIGHT SAVING TIME

NEWS ALERT

OFFICIAL NEWS RELEASE

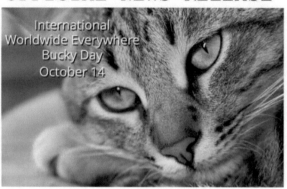

International Worldwide Everywhere Bucky Day October 14

GENEVA - October 14, International Day of the Cat (IDOC), formerly International Cat Day (ICAT), formerly Cats Я Js (CRU), has now been officially changed to International Worldwide Everywhere Bucky Day (IBD).

Recognition of the wide-ranging role of cats (felines) in the daily lives of nearly 1.5 billion* humans worldwide has long been the objective of the International Cat Union, official advocate for kitties.

"I know the renaming of this important day may appear to some as a celebration of just me. Of course, it is, but I share all the praise and adoration with every kitty everywhere," said Bucky (Her Royal Buckyness) in a brief message from her summer residence at historic Buckyness Palace.

"Humans, I appeal to you to heap more love upon the kitty in your home. This love comprises snacks, real food - not from a box or can (Live tuna is best.), lots of toys made from furniture upholstery and limited walks in the garden. A full list of needs may be obtained from the International Cat Union (Not affiliated with any known union) at HRBBuckshot7@gmail. No need to provide your credit card information, we already have it."

Worldwide Everywhere Bucky Day
International Cat Union
Buckyness Palace
Cayman Islands

Unhampered

If you are anything like me, and I believe you are, you want to sleep peacefully knowing your soiled laundry is secure from all threats. Recently, though, things have gone missing. Various examples of the missing objects are shown somewhere near the following punctuation mark. These are the very same photos of missing objects gone missing supplied to our home insurance company, The Great Middle Eastern Hacienda Insurance Company (GMEHIC) headquartered in Milkweed, Idaho.

GMEHIC's 1-800-phone-agent, Penny Hopper Singh, was the acme of kindness, thoughtfulness, professionalism and curiosity, saying, "What you say?"

"Yes. You heard me correctly. Dozens of undergarments of multiple genders have gone missing from my home," I explained.

"I see, sir. Are we talking underwear here?" Ms. Penny inquired.

"Certainly. That's why I am calling GMEHIC."

"Of course. And I am here to help you through this trauma, sir."

"You and GMEHIC are a blessing to my life," I assured Penny.

"What happened exactly? Where did it happen? What time did it happen? What is the value of your loss? Did you file a report with your local police department? I see your policy is set to expire in three days. Can I interest you in upgrading your coverage to

Northern Oklahoma Home Owners Premium Exclusive (NOHOPE)?"

So, I explained. Gave Penny all the information she asked for and that I knew was correct. I had seen enough *Inspector Morse* shows to know how to spell *forensics* and what would be valuable to a serious crime investigation.

It wasn't until I heard a dial tone that I fully comprehended that Ms. Penny had not understood and believed I was most certainly GMEHIC's one-hundredth prank caller of her day.

The rest of the story.

In recent months – for the sake of argument, we'll say 14 months, my Bride and I noticed that we were continually buying underwear - replacements for garments we were certain we already owned.

"But I know I put them in the hamper. That's we always put things that need to travel to the basement laundry," Bride explained.

"I, too, my Bride, appear to have a diminished quantity of undies of late."

Ms. Penny likely believed I was some sort of lonely perv looking to discuss undies, panties and bras with a woman at a toll-free number.

Ms. Penny came to realize Bride and I were serious and that we were victims of theft covered by our home owner policy.

"We estimate the loss of undies at $1200, Ms. Penny," Bride offered.

"Please, call me Ms. Singh."

"Of course."

"Have you now notified the police and filed a report? Complete with dates, times and photos of the alleged crime scene?" Singh asked.

"We have. Sergeant Philips was impressed with the evidence we gave him. He said he might even take it home for further examination. Apparently, there is no Mrs. Sergeant Philips. He's certain the mystery will be solved, though return of our under-treasures remains doubtful," Bride said.

"Excellent," Singh offered. "Please send the photos along with your statement of claim to us here at GMEHIC."

Cold Case Hamper Closed

The great undies heist has been solved. We are now free to give you the details.

Please note that some, all, or none of the illustrations provided as crime scene evidence may be unsuitable for viewers under 18 or over 35 years of age or otherwise incarcerated unless paid subscribers to a social media Internet website paid for by their parents.

Here's how the story unfolded.

OFFICIAL STATE OF CONNECTICUT POLICE EVIDENCE

This evidence report constitutes official or other briefs.
Tampering with briefs may be felony in many jurisdictions.

Police actions in chronological order:

1. Photo: Crime scene geographic location aerial view.
2. Bride and I routinely make deposits to our sky-blue laundry hamper (Action photo unavailable).
3. Photo: Laundry hamper is kept in the master bedroom, usually near a west-facing window in the hope that some ultra-violet sun rays will kill the biggest of the cootie bugs before going into the Maytag. *
4. Photo: Items reported missing.
5. Photo: Most evenings with a former b/Bride. ** Possible clue.
6. Photo: Most evenings with a more recent b/Bride. A definite upgrade. Possible clue.
7. Photo: Bucky stares at TV entertainment center more than might seem appropriate.
8. Cleaning service makes major sweep of house prior our moving to a more underwear-safe city.
9. Photo: Matilda, cleaning service expert moves TV entertainment center. Discovers a trove of underwear behind TV entertainment center just mentioned.

* A German word meaning "Is it morning already."
** It's important to capitalize this word when there is a specific bride in mind.

10. Photo: Authorities find Bucky pretending to be invisible to prevent questioning.
11. Suspect questioned. Continues to profess little knowledge of underwear. "I prefer commando," Bucky said.
12. When authorities confronted Bucky with underwear samples from behind the TV entertainment center covered in kitty fur matching her own, the suspect said, "Oh. That underwear."
13. Bucky taken to the Danbury City jail, paw-printed and released into my custody.
14. A prompt trial before a local magistrate ended in an all-too-expected conviction on a charge of violating Danbury Municipal Code 5681, Abduction of Underwear Against Its Will. Bucky was sentenced to spend one hour in an empty laundry hamper and forfeit one nap.

FORENSICS REPORT

Evidence Exhibit F

Home cleaning expert, Matilda, discovers
missing items behind TV entertainment
center. She is not amused.

FORENSICS REPORT

Missing Property Description

Various undergarments, representing those known to have gone missing.

FORENSICS REPORT

Evidence Exhibit A

Aerial view of alleged crime scene.

Bucky lives here

Alien Spaceship
Landing Zones

FORENSICS REPORT

Evidence Exhibit C

Former bride/Bride ignoring Bucky on sofa
in front of TV entertainment center. Kitty appears unhappy
with her human's selection of mate.

FORENSICS REPORT

Evidence Exhibit E

bride/Bride upgrade pleases Bucky in front of TV entertainment center. Mystery continues.

FORENSICS REPORT
Evidence Exhibit G

Police discover suspect pretending to be invisible. They are not amused.

Danbury Municipal Court Results

Because the accused has no previous convictions,
she is remanded to the custody of her human to spend an hour in an
empty laundry hamper and forfeit one nap.

Always A Puzzle

THE DAWN OF TIME IN LONDON (5:55 A.M. OR 0555 CENTIMETRES).

Since the dawn of time (See photo above.) in London, approximately 5:55 a.m. or 0555 centimetres, cats enjoyed puzzles, not crossword puzzles, but the type humans cling to in times of old age and unemployment. The ones with thousands of oddly-shaped, moveable pieces that mysteriously come together forming a delightful picture of a flower.

Cats, too, enjoy these puzzles, sometimes called "jigsaw puzzles", because of their oddly-shaped, moveable pieces were likely created using a machine known as a jigsaw.

Important to bear in mind, cats like little puzzle pieces. If you are a skilled puzzle maker, you already know this important fact. Beginners, however, too often do not realize just how little and sweet a cat's paws are and make the tragic error of creating puzzles with what are known to professional puzzle cats as "way to large." This was first realized in the late 19th century, 1951, when

149

Wanda Browser used her newly-acquired jigsaw to create a puzzle, that, if successfully assembled, would measure the size of a modern-day Wal-Mart parking lot. Her kitty, Missy, was not impressed and suggested Ms. Browser would pay dearly for her careless error.

"MAYBE A WALL HANGING."

Bucky discovered puzzles when she was just a kitten, age six months, she told me. She took to it like a shark to movies about sharks. How do they even know what a puzzle is at such a tender age? It's baffling, isn't it.

BUCKY, AGE SIX MONTHS

Many theories about this kitty fascination for puzzles float around the human, cat-loving world. Trust me, most are wrong.

If you have the kind of relationship with your kitty that I enjoy and cherish with Bucky, over time, the key to all this will be revealed.

Prevailing assumptions by well-studied persons, many closet dog lovers, about why these sweeties upset your puzzle work in so many annoying ways, suggests several possibilities:

- Cats always push things around because they can.
- Cats are required by their DNA imprinting to annoy humans.
- Cats love to pounce on pretty much anything. It's an exhibit of their ability to seriously damage anything that moves. Things such as mice, insects, Christmas tree ornaments, yarn.

Okay. So. There is some evidence to suggest that some of the above is correct. Though, as a truly dedicated kitty lover, you must understand completely, with all your heart and soul, that the real reason for all this puzzle merriment is the genuine need to be a part of your life for fear you'll hide kitty's favorite napping spots, send her to live with a dog-loving family and/or feed her only dry food from China or Utah.

If you even read any of the early chapters in this collection of magnificent stories, you will recall that I was introduced to Buckshot by Dr. Thumbs Needleman, a super vet from Danbury, Connecticut. Bucky was a casualty of cruelty of the very worst sort and Dr. Needleman saved her life, nursed her to health and found a sucker (me) to adopt her on the spot and spent the following fourteen years loving her, learning from her.

The *Danbury Daily Pancetta* wrote a nice story about it all, (See page 10) crediting Dr. Needleman and very popular Lovely VVO Assistant Victoria Armstrong. I was mentioned as an unidentified Hatter* adopter.

Oh yes. Learning. Puzzles. That's where we left off several lines back.

Like all kitties, Bucky could stare endlessly at a puzzle being assembled on the kitchen table. Not just staring, she explained, but making mental notes. Just how this 45- by 55-inch puzzle was assembled would be key to her work that followed.

BUCKY STUDIES PUZZLE BEFORE ASSEMBLY

"The art and genius of a puzzle," Bucky said, "is in the careful dismantling. We make note of the engineering fact that puzzle pieces often have flat or straight edges. These, we know, will constitute a kind of frame – like a picture frame. So, that's where we start the careful disassembly. When most or many pieces

153

have been placed on the floor, my work is done. It's all a part of wanting to share important life activities with you."

"But, Bucky, sometimes this is very annoying."

"Love is never annoying."

*Hatter is a nickname for someone from Danbury, once known as the hat manufacturing capital of the U.S. Think Stetson (Stock file footnote.).

Princess Buckshot, Her Royal Buckyness, The Buckster, Bucky went home to the Creator Cat in 1998. I feel a tear just at the edge of my eye every day.

The stories will continue.

Afterword

The Book of Bucky may feel like it ends abruptly. It does. But there will be more. Much more.

If you found any part of this exhaustively authoritative and loving tribute to my dear Bucky of value as a love story or as advice or insight into a special relationship you might have with your kitty, please check back often as there will be frequent free updates (FFU) by registering at HRBBuckshot7@gmail.com.

PreLude

As mentioned, five lines above if you were paying attention, *The Book of Bucky* contains much authoritative information, some of which may be viewed as fact. Observation or, as we professional observers like to say, empirical study, presented is true. Only names and facts were changed.

OrdinaryLude

In good conscience, this book was nearly two years in the writing. It could have been written by a less-lazy person in upwards of two weeks.

AfterLude

So much of *The Book of Bucky* was written from actual observations and careful notetaking on scraps of table napkins or, while in Canada, serviettes, over a period of fourteen years. Apologies to all those restaurants.

Post-AfterLude

The Book of Bucky is intended as a love story. HRB Buckshot has been gone some twenty years but not a day has passed without some thought of her. I know pet caregivers and partners fully understand this. We live for them as much as they live for us.

Absolution Request

    The Book of Bucky contains some amazing photographs documenting the life of this sweetie. Many of Bucky's life adventures took place before widespread availability of personal cameras such as the Brownie and Polaroid and the Smartphone. As such, some photographs - and more than you can imagine - contain images of Bucky-like kitties intended to illustrate important historical or educational points. These photographs are fully licensed from Dreamstime, Shutterstock, Pixabay and Wikimedia Commons. Others are the work of the author; you'll be able to easily spot these as they are of inferior quality. Questions about photographs or any other content may be directed to HRBBuckshot7@gmail.com.